MW01489301

AI-102: Designing and implementing a Microsoft Azure AI Solution Certification Exam Guide

Contents

Introduction

Overview of AI-102 Certification

The AI-102: Designing and Implementing a Microsoft Azure AI Solution certification is a specialized credential for professionals aiming to validate their expertise in building, managing, and deploying AI-powered solutions using Microsoft Azure. It demonstrates the ability to leverage Azure AI services to create innovative applications tailored to real-world business needs.

The certification focuses on:

- Designing AI solutions that incorporate computer vision, natural language processing, and conversational AI.
- Implementing AI workflows that scale efficiently while adhering to Microsoft's Responsible AI principles.
- Ensuring security, compliance, and optimization within Azure environments.

Target Audience:
AI Engineers, Solution Architects, Data Scientists, and developers who aim to enhance their skills in Microsoft Azure AI services.

Exam Structure:
The exam typically covers:

1. **Analysis of Solution Requirements (25–30%)**

   Evaluating business needs and identifying AI solutions.

2. **Designing AI Solutions (25–30%)**

   Structuring AI systems with scalability and efficiency.

3. **Implementing and Monitoring AI Solutions (40–45%)**

   Practical aspects of building and managing AI workflows.

Benefits of Certification

1. **Career Advancement:** AI-102 certification enhances your credibility as an Azure AI professional, opening doors to roles such as AI Engineer or AI Solution Architect.
2. **Skill Validation:** It validates your expertise in Microsoft Azure's AI portfolio, boosting your confidence in real-world scenarios.
3. **Competitive Edge:** Organizations value certified professionals for their proven capabilities, making certification a distinguishing factor.
4. **Up-to-Date Knowledge:** Keeping pace with Azure's rapidly evolving ecosystem is vital, and this certification ensures familiarity with the latest tools and best practices.

Exam Prerequisites and Preparation Strategies

To maximize your chances of success, consider the following prerequisites and strategies:

Prerequisites:

- A solid understanding of Python or C#.
- Familiarity with REST APIs and JSON.
- Basic knowledge of machine learning concepts and frameworks.

Preparation Strategies:

1. **Review Official Documentation:** Microsoft Learn offers free resources to understand Azure AI services in-depth.
2. **Hands-On Practice:** Utilize Azure's free tier to practice deploying AI models and managing resources.
3. **Mock Exams:** Take practice tests to identify areas that need improvement.

4. **Study Groups:** Collaborate with peers for knowledge sharing and problem-solving.

Structure of the Book

This book is designed to align with the AI-102 certification syllabus and equip you with practical skills:

- **Part 1:** Fundamentals of Azure AI Solutions.
- **Part 2:** Computer Vision.
- **Part 3:** Natural Language Processing.
- **Part 4:** Conversational AI.
- **Part 5:** Speech Services.
- **Part 6:** Orchestration of AI Workflows.
- **Part 7:** Security and Governance.
- **Part 8:** Case Studies and Practice Tests.

Part 1: Fundamentals of Azure AI Solutions

Chapter 1: Introduction to Microsoft Azure AI

Understanding AI Concepts and Microsoft's AI Offerings

Artificial Intelligence (AI) refers to systems designed to perform tasks that typically require human intelligence, such as decision-making, language understanding, and visual perception. Microsoft Azure leads the AI ecosystem with robust tools and services that cater to these needs.

Key AI Domains in Azure:

1. **Machine Learning (ML):** Tools for building, training, and deploying ML models.

2. **Cognitive Services:** Prebuilt APIs for vision, speech, language, and decision-making.
3. **Bot Framework:** A platform for creating conversational agents.

Microsoft's approach emphasizes democratizing AI with user-friendly tools and Responsible AI principles.

Overview of Azure AI Services

Azure AI Services offer an extensive range of capabilities to develop and deploy intelligent applications. Here's a summary of major offerings:

1. **Azure Cognitive Services:**
   - **Vision:** Analyze images, detect objects, and recognize text.
   - **Speech:** Convert speech to text, synthesize speech, and recognize speakers.
   - **Language:** Perform sentiment analysis, translation, and text summarization.
2. **Azure Machine Learning (Azure ML):**
   A cloud-based platform to build, train, and deploy ML models with tools like AutoML and custom pipelines.
3. **Azure Bot Services:**
   Helps build chatbots that integrate with channels like Teams, Facebook, and more.
4. **Azure Applied AI Services:**
   Offers advanced solutions like Form Recognizer, Video Analyzer, and Azure Cognitive Search.

Setting Up Your Azure Environment

Getting started with Azure AI requires proper environment configuration:

1. **Creating an Azure Account:**
   - Sign up for an Azure free account to access services with a $200 credit.

2. **Configuring Resources:**
   - Use Azure Portal, Azure CLI, or PowerShell to create AI resources.
   - Group related resources for easier management using **Resource Groups**.

3. **Connecting Development Tools:**
   - Install Visual Studio Code or Azure SDKs for seamless development.
   - Set up **Azure Machine Learning Studio** for managing ML workflows.

Azure Resource Management Essentials

Efficient resource management is critical for cost optimization and operational efficiency:

1. **Role-Based Access Control (RBAC):**

   Define roles and permissions to ensure secure access to resources.

2. **Azure Cost Management:**

   Use tools like cost analysis and budgeting to monitor expenses.

3. **Resource Scaling:**

   Optimize resource usage by setting scaling rules for AI workloads.

4. **Monitoring and Logging:**

   Enable Azure Monitor and Application Insights to track performance metrics and diagnose issues.

Chapter 2: AI Workloads and Considerations

AI is revolutionizing industries by enabling organizations to automate processes, gain insights from data, and create intelligent applications. However, successfully implementing AI solutions requires identifying the right workloads, selecting appropriate Azure services, and ensuring the application of ethical and responsible AI principles.

Identifying Suitable AI Workloads

AI workloads vary depending on the domain, business goals, and technological requirements. Choosing suitable workloads involves understanding what AI can achieve and matching those capabilities with organizational needs.

Key AI Workload Categories:

1. **Prediction and Forecasting:**

   AI models can predict future trends based on historical data.

   o Example: Demand forecasting for retail or inventory management.

2. **Classification and Categorization:**

   AI systems categorize data into predefined classes.

   o Example: Email spam filtering or sentiment analysis.

3. **Image and Video Analysis:**

   AI processes visual data to identify patterns, detect objects, or analyze scenes.

   o Example: Face recognition in security systems or defect detection in manufacturing.

4. **Natural Language Processing (NLP):**

   NLP enables AI to understand and generate human language.

- Example: Chatbots for customer service or text summarization for document processing.

5. **Conversational AI:**

   AI powers virtual assistants and chatbots to interact with users naturally.
   - Example: Automating FAQs for technical support.

6. **Speech Recognition and Synthesis:**

   Converting speech to text or vice versa enables hands-free operations.
   - Example: Voice commands in smart home systems or transcription services.

7. **Decision Support Systems:**

   AI aids in complex decision-making by providing insights or recommendations.
   - Example: Fraud detection in banking or personalized recommendations in e-commerce.

Factors for Identifying Suitable Workloads:

- **Data Availability:** Sufficient and relevant data is essential for training AI models.
- **Business Impact:** The workload should align with the organization's strategic objectives.
- **Feasibility:** Evaluate the technical complexity and resource requirements for implementation.
- **Scalability:** Ensure that the AI solution can handle increasing data or user demands.

Choosing the Right Azure Services for AI

Microsoft Azure provides a comprehensive suite of services to address various AI workloads. Choosing the right service requires an understanding of each service's capabilities and how it aligns with your specific workload.

1. Azure Cognitive Services:

Azure Cognitive Services offer prebuilt APIs to integrate AI functionalities into applications without requiring extensive ML expertise.

- **Vision:** For image and video analysis.
    - Services: Computer Vision, Custom Vision, Form Recognizer.
    - Use Case: Automating document processing with OCR.
- **Speech:** For audio processing tasks.
    - Services: Speech-to-Text, Text-to-Speech, Speech Translation.
    - Use Case: Real-time translation for global communication.
- **Language:** For text-based applications.
    - Services: Text Analytics, Translator, Language Understanding (LUIS).
    - Use Case: Sentiment analysis for customer reviews.
- **Decision:** For decision-making and anomaly detection.
    - Services: Personalizer, Anomaly Detector.
    - Use Case: Recommending products based on user behavior.

2. Azure Machine Learning (Azure ML):

A platform for building, training, and deploying custom machine learning models.

- Use Cases: Predictive analytics, custom classification models, and time-series forecasting.
- Tools: AutoML for automated model generation and ML pipelines for workflow orchestration.

3. Azure Bot Services:

Specialized service for developing conversational AI solutions.

- Tools: Bot Framework SDK, Bot Framework Composer.
- Use Cases: Virtual assistants, customer support chatbots.

4. Azure Applied AI Services:

Advanced AI solutions tailored to specific business problems.

- Services: Form Recognizer, Azure Cognitive Search, Metrics Advisor.
- Use Case: Extracting structured data from unstructured documents.

5. Orchestrating AI with Azure Logic Apps:

- Allows automation of workflows by integrating multiple Azure services.
- Use Case: Automating data pipelines between AI services and databases.

Choosing Based on AI Workload:

Workload	Recommended Azure Services
Image Recognition	Computer Vision, Custom Vision
Text Sentiment Analysis	Text Analytics
Conversational AI	Azure Bot Services, LUIS
Predictive Analytics	Azure Machine Learning
Document Processing	Form Recognizer, OCR in Computer Vision

Ethical AI and Responsible AI Guidelines

The adoption of AI comes with ethical challenges. To ensure AI solutions are responsible and beneficial, Microsoft emphasizes principles for Responsible AI.

Principles of Responsible AI:

1. **Fairness:**

   AI systems should treat all individuals and groups equitably.

   - Example: Avoiding biased hiring algorithms.

2. **Reliability and Safety:**

   AI systems must operate reliably and safely under normal and unexpected conditions.

   - Example: Ensuring medical AI does not misdiagnose due to faulty data.

3. **Privacy and Security:**

   Protecting user data and ensuring its confidentiality is paramount.

   - Tools: Azure Key Vault for managing sensitive information.

4. **Inclusiveness:**

   AI solutions should accommodate diverse needs and be accessible to all.

   - Example: Providing screen readers for visually impaired users.

5. **Transparency:**

   Users should understand how AI systems make decisions.

   - Tools: Azure ML's interpretability toolkit for model explainability.

6. **Accountability:**

   Organizations must take responsibility for AI's outcomes.

   - Example: Establishing escalation processes for disputes involving AI systems.

Implementing Responsible AI with Azure Tools:

- **Fairlearn Toolkit:**

  Helps identify and mitigate biases in ML models.

- **InterpretML:**

  Provides insights into how AI models make predictions.

- **Azure Policy:**

  Ensures compliance with regulatory and ethical standards for AI workloads.

- **Monitoring and Auditing:**

- Use Azure Monitor and Application Insights to track AI system performance.
- Audit logs ensure traceability of AI decisions.

Best Practices for Ethical AI Implementation:

- **Data Governance:**
  - Ensure datasets are representative and free from biases.
  - Regularly update datasets to reflect changing real-world conditions.
- **User Consent:**
  - Obtain explicit consent for data usage.
  - Clearly communicate data collection and processing practices.
- **Impact Assessment:**
  - Evaluate the potential societal and environmental impact of AI solutions.
  - Establish protocols for unintended consequences.

Conclusion

AI workloads and considerations are the foundation of successful AI solutions. Identifying suitable workloads ensures that the AI aligns with business goals and technical feasibility. Choosing the right Azure services allows for efficient and scalable implementation. Finally, adhering to Responsible AI principles ensures that solutions are ethical, fair, and transparent, fostering trust and reliability.

This chapter provides the necessary knowledge to start your journey in designing AI systems with Azure. Subsequent chapters will delve into specific AI domains, starting with Computer Vision

Part 2: Implementing Computer Vision Solutions

Chapter 3: Computer Vision Basics with Azure

Computer vision is a subset of artificial intelligence (AI) that enables machines to interpret and analyze visual data from the real world. This capability powers applications such as facial recognition, object detection, image classification, and more. Azure's Computer Vision services make it easy to build and deploy powerful vision solutions for diverse use cases.

Introduction to Azure Computer Vision

Azure Computer Vision is a cloud-based service that provides developers with prebuilt APIs to process and analyze images and videos. It eliminates the need for building complex machine learning (ML) models from scratch, allowing businesses to integrate advanced computer vision capabilities quickly and efficiently.

Key Features of Azure Computer Vision:

1. **Image Analysis:**

   Extract visual features such as objects, faces, colors, and image types.

   - Example: Detecting objects in a product catalog.

2. **Optical Character Recognition (OCR):**

   Extract text from images or documents, including handwritten text.

   - Example: Automating data entry from scanned forms.

3. **Custom Vision:**

   Train custom ML models for specific image classification or object detection tasks.

   - Example: Identifying product defects in a manufacturing pipeline.

4. **Face API:**

   Detect and analyze facial features, recognize emotions, and match faces.

   - Example: Enabling secure access through facial authentication.

5. **Video Indexer:**

   Analyze videos to extract metadata, detect scenes, and recognize spoken content.

   - Example: Indexing corporate training videos for searchability.

Benefits of Azure Computer Vision:

- **Scalability:** Process thousands of images efficiently using Azure's infrastructure.
- **Ease of Use:** Pretrained models enable quick implementation without extensive ML expertise.

- **Integration:** Seamlessly integrates with other Azure services such as Azure Blob Storage and Azure Cognitive Search.
- **Global Reach:** Available in multiple regions and supports various languages for OCR.

Image Analysis and Object Detection

Image analysis is one of the most powerful applications of computer vision. It involves extracting meaningful information from visual content, such as identifying objects, detecting colors, or recognizing faces. Azure Computer Vision simplifies these tasks through its Image Analysis API.

How Image Analysis Works

The Image Analysis API processes an input image and returns structured data containing:

- **Tags:** High-level descriptions of objects or scenes in the image.
- **Categories:** Broad classifications of the image content.
- **Objects:** Detailed information about detected objects, including bounding boxes.
- **Description:** Natural language captions summarizing the image.
- **Faces:** Details like age, gender, and facial landmarks.
- **Color Scheme:** Information about dominant and accent colors.

Use Case: Automating Inventory Management

Consider a retailer automating inventory tracking:

- Images of shelves are captured at regular intervals.

- The Image Analysis API identifies products and determines which items need restocking.
- Integration with Power BI generates real-time inventory reports.

Implementing Image Analysis

1. **Set Up the Azure Computer Vision Resource:**
   - Create a resource in the Azure portal.
   - Retrieve the API key and endpoint URL.

2. **Write Code for Analysis:**

   Use Python or another SDK-supported language:

   python

   Copy code

   ```python
   from azure.cognitiveservices.vision.computervision import ComputerVisionClient
   from msrest.authentication import CognitiveServicesCredentials

   # Authentication
   client = ComputerVisionClient(
       endpoint="YOUR_ENDPOINT",
       credentials=CognitiveServicesCredentials("YOUR_API_KEY")
   )

   # Analyze Image
   image_url = "https://example.com/image.jpg"
   analysis = client.analyze_image(image_url, visual_features=["Categories", "Tags", "Objects"])
   for tag in analysis.tags:
       print(f"Tag: {tag.name}, Confidence: {tag.confidence}")
   ```

Custom Vision, a subset of Azure Computer Vision, allows you to train models tailored to specific object detection tasks.

Steps to Train a Custom Vision Model:

1. **Create a Custom Vision Resource:**
   - Use the Azure portal or CLI to set up the resource.
2. **Upload Training Data:**
   - Upload labeled images with bounding boxes for object detection.
3. **Train the Model:**
   - Use the Custom Vision portal to train and evaluate the model.
4. **Deploy the Model:**
   - Export the trained model to an Azure service or on-premises environment.

Extracting Text with Optical Character Recognition (OCR)

Optical Character Recognition (OCR) is a crucial capability of Azure Computer Vision that extracts text from images, scanned documents, and handwritten notes. OCR is widely used for digitizing information and automating manual data entry.

Capabilities of Azure OCR

1. **Printed Text Recognition:**

   Extracts text from images containing printed characters.
   - Example: Reading invoice details from scanned PDFs.
2. **Handwritten Text Recognition:**

   Detects and converts handwritten notes into digital text.

- o   Example: Digitizing meeting notes for storage and analysis.

3. **Multilanguage Support:**

   Recognizes text in over 25 languages, making it suitable for global
   applications.

4. **Layout Analysis:**

   Extracts text while preserving the layout, useful for structured documents.

Use Case: Automating Document Processing

Consider an insurance company processing claims forms:

- Scanned forms are uploaded to Azure Blob Storage.
- The OCR API extracts text fields such as name, policy number, and claim
  details.
- Extracted data is stored in a database for further processing.

Implementing OCR

1. **Set Up the Computer Vision Resource:**

   Follow the same setup process as for Image Analysis.

2. **Code Example:**

   Use Python to extract text from an image:

```python
Copy code
from azure.cognitiveservices.vision.computervision import
ComputerVisionClient
from msrest.authentication import CognitiveServicesCredentials

# Authentication
client = ComputerVisionClient(
    endpoint="YOUR_ENDPOINT",
```

```python
        credentials=CognitiveServicesCredentials("YOUR_API_KEY")
    )

    # Perform OCR
    image_url = "https://example.com/document.jpg"
    ocr_results = client.read(image_url, raw=True)
    operation_location = ocr_results.headers["Operation-Location"]
    operation_id = operation_location.split("/")[-1]

    # Get Results
    results = client.get_read_result(operation_id)
    if results.status == "succeeded":
        for page in results.analyze_result.read_results:
            for line in page.lines:
                print(line.text)
```

Handling Complex Documents with Form Recognizer

Azure Form Recognizer extends OCR capabilities by extracting structured data from complex documents.

- Use Case: Extracting fields such as invoice numbers, dates, and amounts from financial documents.
- Advantage: Pretrained models minimize manual effort for template design.

Conclusion

Azure Computer Vision empowers developers to implement image analysis, object detection, and OCR capabilities with minimal effort. By leveraging prebuilt APIs and customizable models, businesses can build intelligent solutions tailored to their needs. This chapter laid the foundation for working with computer vision on Azure. The next chapter will delve deeper into custom vision scenarios and advanced applications.

Chapter 4: Advanced Vision Scenarios

As artificial intelligence (AI) and computer vision technologies continue to evolve, the demand for more customized, advanced, and complex vision solutions grows. Azure Cognitive Services provides several tools that allow developers and businesses to build tailored computer vision applications with greater flexibility and efficiency. In this chapter, we will explore advanced vision scenarios using Azure's **Custom Vision**, **Form Recognizer**, and other tools. These solutions will help you address more specific needs and challenges in industries like healthcare, retail, manufacturing, and finance.

Custom Vision with Azure Cognitive Services

Custom Vision is a key feature of Azure Cognitive Services that allows businesses to create custom image classification and object detection models to meet their specific needs. Unlike the prebuilt models in standard computer vision APIs, **Custom Vision** gives users the flexibility to tailor models to recognize their unique objects or images based on their data.

Azure's **Custom Vision** service provides two main functionalities:

1. **Image Classification** – The ability to classify an image into one or more categories. For example, recognizing whether an image contains a cat, dog, or bird.
2. **Object Detection** – Identifying specific objects in an image and providing the exact location (bounding box) of the object.

Custom Vision is particularly useful when you need a model trained on your specific dataset, as out-of-the-box models might not recognize highly specialized objects.

Benefits of Using Custom Vision

- **Tailored Models:** Create models that can classify or detect objects unique to your business or use case.
- **No Deep Learning Expertise Required:** Azure provides a user-friendly interface for training and testing models, making it accessible to both developers and non-experts.
- **Fast Training:** Azure Custom Vision allows you to upload images, train models, and deploy them quickly, reducing the time to go from concept to implementation.
- **Scalability:** Custom Vision models can be easily deployed at scale with Azure's cloud infrastructure, allowing you to manage and serve models across multiple devices and platforms.

Training and Deploying Custom Vision Models

In this section, we will walk through the key steps of training and deploying custom vision models on Azure.

Step 1: Create an Azure Custom Vision Resource

To begin using Azure Custom Vision, you need to first create a **Custom Vision** resource in the Azure portal.

- **Log into the Azure portal** and create a new Custom Vision resource.
- After creating the resource, you'll receive a **Key** and **Endpoint**, which are needed to authenticate requests to the service.

Step 2: Preparing Your Data

Before you can train a model, you need to prepare the images. This is a crucial step in ensuring the success of your custom vision model.

- **Collect Images:** You will need a substantial dataset of labeled images. The more diverse the dataset, the more accurate your model will be. For example, if you're creating a model to classify different types of fruits, you should gather images of each fruit from various angles, lighting conditions, and backgrounds.
- **Label Images:** Each image in your dataset must be tagged with labels that represent what the model should recognize. This process is called **annotation**. You can use the **Azure Custom Vision portal** to label images manually or use an external tool to label them in bulk.
- **Image Types:** Custom Vision supports image files in popular formats like JPEG, PNG, and GIF.

Step 3: Training the Model

With the data prepared, you can begin the process of **training** your custom model.

- **Upload Labeled Images:** Once your images are labeled, upload them to the Azure Custom Vision portal.
- **Choose Model Type:** You can choose to train either an **image classification model** or an **object detection model**, depending on your needs.
  - **Image Classification:** Used when you want to classify an entire image (e.g., "cat" or "dog").
  - **Object Detection:** Used when you need to identify and localize multiple objects within an image.
- **Train Model:** After uploading your images and selecting your model type, click on **Train**. The Azure platform will use your images and labels to build and train a model. This process typically takes just a few minutes.
- **Evaluation:** Once trained, you can test the model's accuracy by using a separate set of images that were not part of the training dataset (commonly called a **validation set**).

Step 4: Deploying the Model

Once you have trained and tested the model, it's time to deploy it.

- **Deployment Options:** Azure offers several deployment options for your Custom Vision model.
  - **Cloud Deployment:** Deploy the model as a cloud-based service. This allows you to easily integrate your model into other cloud applications.
  - **Edge Deployment:** Deploy your model to local devices such as smartphones, IoT devices, or edge devices. Azure provides SDKs for several platforms, including iOS, Android, and Raspberry Pi.
- **APIs and SDKs:** Use the provided **REST APIs** or the SDKs (Python, C#, etc.) to integrate your trained model into your applications.

Once deployed, you can continue to monitor the performance of your model and gather feedback. If you find that certain objects are being misclassified or not detected properly, you can retrain the model by adding new labeled images and repeating the training process. Custom Vision also allows you to **fine-tune** models over time to ensure they improve as new data comes in.

Leveraging Form Recognizer for Document Processing

One of the most exciting advanced capabilities of Azure Cognitive Services is **Form Recognizer**. This tool simplifies document processing by automating data extraction from scanned documents, forms, receipts, and invoices. Form Recognizer uses machine learning models to understand the structure of documents and extract meaningful data without the need for manual data entry.

What is Form Recognizer?

Form Recognizer is an AI-powered document extraction tool that automates the process of converting scanned documents into structured data. It uses machine learning to analyze the content, layout, and formatting of documents and can extract key-value pairs, tables, and text fields.

Key Features of Form Recognizer

1. **Prebuilt Models:**
    - **Receipt Model:** Extracts data from receipts, such as vendor name, total amount, date, and more.
    - **Invoice Model:** Automatically detects fields like invoice number, billing address, date, and line items.

- o **Business Card Model:** Extracts contact information from business cards.

2. **Custom Models:**

   - o **Custom Form Recognizer:** You can train a custom model to extract information from specific types of documents (e.g., contracts, insurance forms) that don't follow standard formats.

3. **Table Extraction:**

   - o Form Recognizer can recognize and extract structured data from tables in scanned documents or PDFs. It captures not only the data but also the relationship between cells, rows, and columns, which is essential for proper data analysis.

4. **Document Layout Analysis:**

   - o It understands the layout of the document, such as paragraphs, headers, footers, and other formatting structures.

How Form Recognizer Works

Form Recognizer works by extracting information from a document through several key steps:

1. **Upload Document:** Upload a document (e.g., a PDF or image file) to the Azure Form Recognizer API.

2. **Form Processing:** Form Recognizer's prebuilt or custom models process the document and analyze its structure.

3. **Data Extraction:** The tool identifies key-value pairs, tables, and other relevant information in the document. It then returns the structured data in a JSON format.

Consider an invoice processing scenario. By leveraging Form Recognizer, a company can automate its invoice processing pipeline:

1. **Document Upload:** Scanned invoices are uploaded to Azure Blob Storage.
2. **Data Extraction:** Form Recognizer's Invoice Model processes the documents and extracts key information such as the invoice number, vendor details, date, and line items.
3. **Data Integration:** Extracted data is automatically integrated into an enterprise resource planning (ERP) system or database.
4. **Workflow Automation:** After the data is extracted, workflows for approval, payment, and filing are automatically triggered.

Form Recognizer API Example

Here's how you can interact with Form Recognizer using Python:

```python
Copy code
from azure.ai.formrecognizer import DocumentAnalysisClient
from azure.core.credentials import AzureKeyCredential

# Instantiate the client
endpoint = "https://<your-endpoint>.cognitiveservices.azure.com/"
key = "<your-api-key>"
client = DocumentAnalysisClient(endpoint=endpoint,
credential=AzureKeyCredential(key))

# Upload document
document_url = "https://example.com/invoice.pdf"
```

```
poller = client.begin_analyze_document_from_url("prebuilt-invoice", document_url)
result = poller.result()

# Extract data from result
for document in result.documents:
    for field_name, field_value in document.fields.items():
        print(f"{field_name}: {field_value.value}")
```

Use Cases for Form Recognizer

1. **Automating Accounts Payable:** Extracting and processing invoice data automatically from invoices to streamline the accounts payable process.

2. **Document Archiving:** Digitizing and extracting key information from legal contracts or business agreements to organize and store them in a searchable database.

3. **Healthcare Form Processing:** Automating the extraction of patient data from medical forms to improve the efficiency of healthcare operations.

Conclusion

In this chapter, we explored advanced vision scenarios using Azure's **Custom Vision** and **Form Recognizer**. These powerful tools allow you to create tailored vision solutions for a variety of use cases, from custom object detection and image classification to automating document processing. By leveraging these services, organizations can improve operational efficiency, reduce manual effort, and implement cutting-edge AI solutions.

Part 3: Working with Natural Language Processing (NLP)

Chapter 5: Introduction to Azure NLP Services

Natural Language Processing (NLP) has revolutionized the way machines interpret, understand, and respond to human language. NLP is a subfield of artificial intelligence (AI) that focuses on the interaction between computers and human language. It encompasses a variety of tasks, including language translation, sentiment analysis, entity recognition, and text summarization. In recent years, cloud platforms like Microsoft Azure have emerged as critical enablers of advanced NLP capabilities, allowing businesses to build sophisticated language models without requiring deep expertise in linguistics or machine learning.

In this chapter, we will explore the fundamentals of Natural Language Processing and dive into **Azure NLP Services**, focusing particularly on **Text Analytics** for tasks like sentiment analysis and key phrase extraction. These tools empower developers and organizations to create applications that understand, analyze, and process human language effectively.

Natural Language Processing Fundamentals

NLP involves a series of processes that help a machine interpret and respond to text or speech data in a way that mimics human language comprehension. The challenge of NLP lies in the vast complexity of human language, which includes nuances such as grammar, context, and ambiguity.

Key NLP Concepts:

- **Tokenization:** The process of breaking down text into smaller units, like words or sentences. For example, in the sentence "I love AI," tokenization would break it into ["I", "love", "AI"].
- **Part-of-Speech Tagging:** Assigning word classes (e.g., noun, verb, adjective) to each token in a sentence to help understand its grammatical structure.

- **Named Entity Recognition (NER):** Identifying and categorizing key entities in a text, such as names of people, organizations, dates, or locations.
- **Dependency Parsing:** Analyzing the grammatical structure of a sentence and establishing relationships between words (e.g., which noun a verb is associated with).
- **Stemming and Lemmatization:** Reducing words to their base forms. For example, "running" becomes "run" in stemming and "better" becomes "good" in lemmatization.
- **Stop Words Removal:** Filtering out common words like "the", "and", and "is" that carry little meaning in text analysis.

The application of these techniques enables various NLP tasks, such as:

- **Sentiment Analysis:** Determining the emotional tone behind a text, whether positive, negative, or neutral.
- **Text Classification:** Categorizing text into predefined labels (e.g., spam detection).
- **Language Translation:** Converting text from one language to another.
- **Question Answering:** Building systems that can answer questions based on a provided context.

NLP can be implemented using several machine learning algorithms, including traditional methods (e.g., Naive Bayes, Support Vector Machines) and deep learning models (e.g., LSTM, BERT).

Applications of NLP

- **Customer Service:** Automating responses to customer inquiries through chatbots or virtual assistants.
- **Social Media Analysis:** Analyzing user posts or comments to detect sentiment or identify trends.

- **Healthcare:** Extracting important medical information from patient records and clinical notes.
- **Finance:** Monitoring financial news to detect potential risks or investment opportunities.

Using Text Analytics for Sentiment Analysis and Key Phrase Extraction

Microsoft Azure provides a powerful suite of **Text Analytics** tools that allow developers to easily implement common NLP tasks such as **sentiment analysis, key phrase extraction, language detection**, and **entity recognition**. These prebuilt models help save time and resources by automating the interpretation of textual data without requiring extensive data science knowledge.

Text Analytics API Overview

Azure's **Text Analytics API** is a cloud-based service that provides language processing capabilities through simple RESTful APIs. The Text Analytics API offers a wide range of NLP functionalities, including:

1. **Sentiment Analysis:** Determines whether the sentiment of a piece of text is positive, neutral, or negative.
2. **Key Phrase Extraction:** Identifies and extracts important phrases from a text that best represent the main ideas.
3. **Language Detection:** Identifies the language of a text.
4. **Named Entity Recognition (NER):** Recognizes entities such as people, organizations, and locations in a text.
5. **PII Detection (Personally Identifiable Information):** Detects sensitive personal information like credit card numbers and phone numbers in text.

In this section, we will focus on how to use Azure's Text Analytics API for two specific tasks: **sentiment analysis** and **key phrase extraction**.

Sentiment Analysis

Sentiment analysis is one of the most widely used NLP tasks. It involves determining the sentiment or emotional tone behind a given text. The sentiment can typically be classified into three categories:

- **Positive:** The text expresses a favorable or optimistic sentiment.
- **Negative:** The text expresses an unfavorable or pessimistic sentiment.
- **Neutral:** The text has a neutral or balanced sentiment with no clear positive or negative inclination.

Sentiment analysis is useful for a variety of applications, including:

- **Brand Monitoring:** Analyzing social media or customer reviews to gauge public sentiment about a product or service.
- **Customer Service:** Automatically categorizing customer feedback to prioritize issues based on sentiment.
- **Market Research:** Analyzing news articles or surveys to detect public opinions on a particular topic or event.

How Sentiment Analysis Works in Azure

Azure's Text Analytics API analyzes text and returns a sentiment score between 0 and 1, where:

- **1** represents a highly positive sentiment.
- **0** represents a highly negative sentiment.

In addition to the sentiment score, the API also provides an overall sentiment classification (positive, neutral, or negative).

Let's consider a scenario where a company wants to analyze customer feedback to understand the sentiment of user reviews for a product.

1. **Set Up Text Analytics Resource in Azure:**
   - Log into the Azure portal and create a new **Text Analytics** resource.
   - Retrieve the **API Key** and **Endpoint**.
2. **Code Example:** Here is an example of how to use the **Text Analytics API** to analyze sentiment using Python.

python

Copy code

```python
from azure.ai.textanalytics import TextAnalyticsClient
from azure.core.credentials import AzureKeyCredential


# Initialize the client
key = "YOUR_API_KEY"
endpoint = "YOUR_ENDPOINT"
client = TextAnalyticsClient(endpoint=endpoint, credential=AzureKeyCredential(key))


# Text data
documents = [
    "I absolutely love this product! It works wonders and is easy to use.",
    "The product is okay, but I had a few issues with it.",
    "I hate this product. It broke after one use and the customer service is terrible."
]


# Sentiment Analysis
response = client.analyze_sentiment(documents)
```

```
# Print results
for idx, document in enumerate(response):
    print(f"Document {idx + 1}: Sentiment = {document.sentiment}")
    print(f"Scores: Positive = {document.confidence_scores.positive}, Negative =
{document.confidence_scores.negative}, Neutral =
{document.confidence_scores.neutral}")
```

The output will categorize each document's sentiment, providing a sentiment label (positive, neutral, or negative) along with confidence scores.

Key Phrase Extraction

Key phrase extraction is another essential NLP task in which the goal is to identify the most relevant or significant phrases within a text. Key phrases help summarize the main points of a document or highlight the most important aspects of the content.

Key phrase extraction is useful for:

- **Content Summarization:** Automatically generating summaries of articles, blog posts, or documents.
- **Search Engine Optimization (SEO):** Identifying important keywords in content to improve search ranking.
- **Data Categorization:** Extracting important terms from datasets for further analysis or organization.

How Key Phrase Extraction Works in Azure

Azure's Text Analytics API provides a straightforward way to extract key phrases from text. The API analyzes the input text and returns a list of important terms or phrases that represent the core content of the document.

Let's say you want to extract the key phrases from a news article or research paper.

1. **Set Up Text Analytics Resource in Azure:**
   - Similar to sentiment analysis, set up your Text Analytics resource in the Azure portal and obtain the **API Key** and **Endpoint**.
2. **Code Example:** Here's an example in Python for extracting key phrases:

python

Copy code

```python
from azure.ai.textanalytics import TextAnalyticsClient
from azure.core.credentials import AzureKeyCredential

# Initialize the client
key = "YOUR_API_KEY"
endpoint = "YOUR_ENDPOINT"
client = TextAnalyticsClient(endpoint=endpoint, credential=AzureKeyCredential(key))

# Text data
documents = [
    "Azure is a cloud computing service created by Microsoft, offering a range of services including data analytics, machine learning, and more.",
    "Natural language processing is a critical aspect of AI and allows for the understanding of human language through machines."
]

# Extract Key Phrases
response = client.extract_key_phrases(documents)
```

```
# Print results
for idx, document in enumerate(response):
    print(f"Document {idx + 1}: Key Phrases = {', '.join(document.key_phrases)}")
```

The output will display the key phrases extracted from each document.

Real-World Use Case: Content Recommendation

Key phrase extraction can also be used in content recommendation systems. For example, a news website could extract key phrases from articles to recommend similar content to users based on their reading habits. This can be done by comparing key phrases between articles and suggesting similar ones.

Conclusion

In this chapter, we have introduced the fundamentals of Natural Language Processing (NLP) and demonstrated how to use **Azure Text Analytics** for sentiment analysis and key phrase extraction. By leveraging Azure's powerful NLP services, developers and businesses can create intelligent applications that understand and process human language with ease.

These NLP tools—along with others in Azure's suite of services—provide powerful capabilities for automating text analysis, improving customer experiences, and extracting actionable insights from vast amounts of unstructured data. By integrating these tools into real-world applications, organizations can gain a deeper understanding of customer feedback, content, and more, driving informed decision-making and operational efficiency.

Chapter 6: Building Custom NLP Models

In this chapter, we will explore the process of building custom Natural Language Processing (NLP) models using Microsoft Azure's advanced tools and services. Custom NLP models are essential for developing tailored solutions that address specific business needs, from conversational agents to multilingual applications. We will cover three key Azure services that empower you to create robust NLP models:

1. **Language Understanding (LUIS)**: A service that enables you to build custom language models to interpret user input effectively.
2. **Azure Bot Services**: A platform for designing, developing, and deploying intelligent conversational agents or chatbots.
3. **Azure Translator**: A service that allows you to add translation capabilities to applications, enabling multilingual support for users across the globe.

Together, these services help you create powerful, intelligent applications that understand, respond to, and translate natural language inputs. By the end of this chapter, you will be equipped with the knowledge to design custom NLP models that meet the unique demands of your organization and user base.

Working with Language Understanding (LUIS)

Language Understanding Intelligent Service (LUIS) is a cloud-based service from Microsoft that helps developers create custom NLP models for understanding natural language inputs. LUIS allows developers to build applications that can understand user intents, recognize entities, and take actions based on natural language commands.

LUIS simplifies the process of training a machine learning model for language understanding, without requiring deep expertise in machine learning or NLP.

Key Concepts in LUIS:

1. **Intents**: Intents represent the user's purpose or goal. For example, if a user says "book a flight," the intent is to **BookFlight**.
2. **Entities**: Entities are specific pieces of information in the user's input that help to clarify the intent. For example, in the sentence "Book a flight from New York to London," "New York" and "London" are entities, and the intent is **BookFlight**.
3. **Utterances**: Utterances are examples of the input phrases that users might say to invoke a particular intent. For instance, "Reserve a seat from New York to London" is an utterance for the **BookFlight** intent.

Creating a LUIS Application

1. **Setting Up LUIS:**
   o To start working with LUIS, you first need to create a LUIS resource in the Azure portal. This involves setting up a subscription and creating a LUIS app.
   o Once your app is created, LUIS provides a web-based interface where you can train and test your model.
2. **Training a LUIS Model:**

- **Define Intents**: First, you will define the types of user intents. For example, if you are building a flight booking application, you might define intents like **BookFlight**, **CancelFlight**, and **CheckFlightStatus**.
- **Label Entities**: Next, you will identify and label entities within your utterances. For example, in the utterance "Book a flight from New York to London," the entities would be **New York** (departure city) and **London** (destination city).
- **Provide Examples**: LUIS works by learning from labeled examples. You provide multiple variations of user input to teach LUIS how to recognize intents and entities accurately.
- **Train and Test**: After defining intents and labeling entities, you train the model using the training data and test it with different utterances to ensure it understands the user input correctly.

3. **Integrating LUIS with Applications:**
   - After training and testing, you can publish the model and integrate it with your applications using the LUIS API. This allows your application to interpret user input and respond appropriately.
   - The LUIS API provides real-time prediction, returning the identified intent and entities along with a confidence score.

Example: Flight Booking with LUIS

Consider an example where you build a chatbot to help users book flights. Here's how LUIS can be used:

- **Intents**:
  - **BookFlight**
  - **CheckFlightStatus**
  - **CancelFlight**
- **Entities**:

- DepartureCity
- DestinationCity
- FlightDate

For the input "Book a flight from New York to London on January 5th", LUIS will identify:

- **Intent**: **BookFlight**
- **Entities**: **New York** (DepartureCity), **London** (DestinationCity), **January 5th** (FlightDate)

This information is then passed to the backend system, which processes the request and books the flight.

Designing Conversational AI with Azure Bot Services

Azure Bot Services offers a platform for designing, building, and deploying intelligent chatbots. These bots can interact with users through natural language, using services like LUIS for language understanding and Azure Cognitive Services for additional capabilities such as speech recognition and image analysis.

Azure Bot Services leverages the **Bot Framework**, which includes a set of tools, libraries, and services that help developers create conversational experiences across various channels, including web apps, mobile apps, social media platforms (like Facebook Messenger and Slack), and voice assistants (like Microsoft Cortana and Amazon Alexa).

Key Concepts in Azure Bot Services:

1. **Bot Framework SDK**: The Bot Framework SDK provides libraries to build bots using various programming languages like C#, JavaScript, and Python. The SDK

supports the development of bots with features like dialogs, state management, and adaptive dialogs.

2. **Dialogs**: A dialog is a component that represents a conversation between the user and the bot. Dialogs manage the flow of conversation, guiding the user through different steps based on their inputs.

3. **Bot Channels**: Azure Bot Services supports integration with various messaging platforms. These channels include popular communication platforms like Microsoft Teams, Facebook Messenger, WhatsApp, and more.

4. **Bot Services Integration**: Bots can integrate with other Azure services, such as LUIS for NLP, QnA Maker for knowledge bases, and Cognitive Services for tasks like image recognition, sentiment analysis, and speech synthesis.

Steps to Build a Conversational Bot:

1. **Create a Bot Resource in Azure**:
   - Navigate to the Azure portal and create a new **Bot Services** resource.
   - Configure the bot by selecting the programming language and desired features.

2. **Develop the Bot**:
   - Use the **Bot Framework SDK** to create the bot's logic. You will define how the bot handles user inputs, guides conversations, and responds to specific intents.
   - Implement dialogs to manage the flow of conversation. For instance, if the user wants to book a flight, the bot will ask for the destination, date, and other necessary details.

3. **Integrate LUIS with the Bot**:
   - LUIS can be integrated into your bot to recognize intents and entities in user inputs. For example, if the user says, "Book a flight from Chicago to Miami," LUIS will extract the **BookFlight** intent and **Chicago** and **Miami** as entities.

- The bot can then process the user's request by interacting with backend systems or databases.

4. **Deploy the Bot**:
   - Once the bot is developed, you can deploy it to various platforms like Microsoft Teams, Slack, or Facebook Messenger. Azure Bot Services makes deployment easy with built-in support for a variety of channels.

Example: Flight Booking Bot

Consider a bot that helps users book flights. The conversation might look like this:

1. User: "I want to book a flight."
2. Bot: "Sure! Where would you like to fly from?"
3. User: "Chicago."
4. Bot: "Great! Where are you flying to?"
5. User: "Miami."
6. Bot: "When would you like to fly?"
7. User: "January 5th."
8. Bot: "Booking your flight from Chicago to Miami on January 5th."

In this scenario, the bot integrates with **LUIS** to identify the intent **BookFlight** and the entities **Chicago**, **Miami**, and **January 5th**.

Implementing Translator for Multilingual Applications

Azure Translator is a cloud-based service that enables developers to add translation capabilities to their applications. It supports over 70 languages and allows for text translation, real-time speech translation, and even document translation. Translator can be used to build multilingual applications that cater to users from diverse linguistic backgrounds.

Key Features of Azure Translator:

1. **Text Translation**: The Translator API provides real-time translation between supported languages. This service is useful for chat applications, customer service platforms, or global websites.

2. **Speech Translation**: The speech translation service enables speech-to-text translation. It's ideal for applications that require real-time multilingual communication, such as video conferencing or customer support centers.

3. **Document Translation**: This feature enables you to translate entire documents while preserving their formatting. This is useful for translating contracts, reports, and other complex documents.

4. **Language Detection**: The Translator API can automatically detect the language of the input text, making it easy to handle multilingual input from users.

5. **Custom Translation**: You can also customize the translation model to suit your specific needs, ensuring that translations are accurate for your industry or domain.

How to Use Translator in Applications:

1. **Set Up Translator in Azure**:
   - Create a Translator resource in the Azure portal and obtain the API key and endpoint.

2. **Translate Text**:
   - Once set up, you can use the Translator API to translate text between languages. The API supports batch translation, which is useful for translating large volumes of text.

3. **Integrate Translator with Chatbots**:
   - If you are building a multilingual chatbot, you can integrate Translator to dynamically translate user inputs and responses.

  ○ For example, if a French-speaking user asks a question in French, the chatbot can automatically translate it into English, process the request, and then translate the response back into French.

Example: Translating User Input in a Chatbot

1. User: "Je veux réserver un vol" (French for "I want to book a flight").
2. Bot: Translates the input to English using the Translator API.
3. Bot: Processes the request and responds: "Where would you like to fly from?"
4. User: "Chicago."
5. Bot: Translates the response back into French.

This seamless integration of translation allows businesses to provide multilingual support to users, regardless of their location or language.

Conclusion

In this chapter, we have explored three essential services for building custom NLP models and solutions using Microsoft Azure: **Language Understanding (LUIS)**, **Azure Bot Services**, and **Azure Translator**.

- **LUIS** allows developers to build custom language models that can understand user intents and entities, enabling intelligent decision-making.
- **Azure Bot Services** enables the creation of sophisticated conversational agents that can interact with users through natural language, across various platforms and channels.
- **Azure Translator** opens the door to multilingual applications, allowing businesses to provide seamless communication across different languages.

By leveraging these powerful tools, developers can create intelligent, multilingual, and conversational applications that understand and respond to human language in ways that were previously impossible. These services enable businesses to deliver more personalized, efficient, and inclusive experiences for their users.

Chapter 7: Introduction to Azure Bot Service

In this chapter, we will dive deep into **Azure Bot Service**, which is a comprehensive suite of tools, services, and frameworks that allows developers to build intelligent, conversational AI applications. Whether you are looking to create a simple chatbot or a sophisticated conversational agent, Azure Bot Service provides the necessary tools and infrastructure to develop, test, deploy, and scale your chatbot applications.

We'll cover the following key topics in this chapter:

1. **Building and Deploying a Basic Chatbot**: Learn how to create a simple chatbot that can interact with users and perform tasks.
2. **Integrating Bots with Channels**: Understand how to extend your chatbot's reach by integrating it with popular messaging platforms like Microsoft Teams, Web Chat, Facebook Messenger, and more.
3. **Understanding Dialogs and State Management**: Explore how to structure conversations and manage user interactions with dialogs and state management within Azure Bot Service.

By the end of this chapter, you will have the skills to build a functional chatbot, integrate it with different communication channels, and manage its conversational flow with dialogs and state management features.

Building and Deploying a Basic Chatbot

Azure Bot Service offers a comprehensive development environment for building, deploying, and managing chatbots. It provides a cloud-based infrastructure where developers can create bots using the **Bot Framework SDK** and manage these bots with minimal hassle.

Steps to Build a Basic Chatbot Using Azure Bot Service:

1. **Create an Azure Bot Service Resource**:
   - To begin, you need an **Azure account** and access to the **Azure portal**. After logging into the Azure portal, create a **Bot Services** resource.

- o Select the **Web App Bot** template, which simplifies the process of creating and deploying a bot.
- o You will be prompted to provide basic information such as the bot's name, resource group, and region.

2. **Choose a Development Language**:
   - o Azure Bot Service supports several programming languages, including **C#, JavaScript, Python**, and **Java**. You can choose your preferred language based on the development environment you're comfortable with.
   - o If you are using the **Bot Framework SDK**, you can build the bot either using **Bot Framework Composer** (a visual tool for creating bots) or by coding manually using the SDK.

3. **Developing the Bot's Core Logic**:
   - o The bot's core logic determines how it will interact with users. Using the Bot Framework SDK, you can define the different intents and actions your bot will take when users ask questions or issue commands.
   - o You can begin by creating a simple **Echo Bot**, where the bot replies with the same message it receives from the user. This is a simple yet effective way to get started and understand how the bot framework works.

Here's an example of a basic **Echo Bot** in **C#**:

```csharp
Copy code
public class EchoBot : ActivityHandler
{
    protected override async Task
OnMessageActivityAsync(ITurnContext<IMessageActivity> turnContext,
CancellationToken cancellationToken)
```

```
    {
        // Echo the user's message back
        await turnContext.SendActivityAsync(MessageFactory.Text($"You said:
{turnContext.Activity.Text}"), cancellationToken);
    }
}
```

This bot simply listens for a message and echoes it back to the user.

4. **Testing the Bot**:
   - After implementing the core functionality, you can test your bot locally using the **Bot Framework Emulator**. The Emulator is a desktop application that allows you to simulate interactions with your bot, test its responses, and debug any issues in the development process.
   - Once you're satisfied with the functionality, you can publish the bot to Azure.

5. **Deploying the Bot**:
   - After testing the bot locally, you can deploy it to Azure. The Azure Bot Service automatically handles the hosting, scaling, and management of the bot's infrastructure, so you can focus on the bot's functionality.
   - Deployment is simple with a **one-click** process in the Azure portal, or you can automate the deployment through continuous integration (CI) pipelines in Azure DevOps.

Example Interaction:

User: "Hello, bot!" Bot: "You said: Hello, bot!"

This is the foundation of many chatbots. You can expand this functionality to perform more complex tasks like booking appointments, answering customer queries, and more.

Integrating Bots with Channels

Once you have developed your chatbot, it's time to make it available to users across different platforms. Azure Bot Service supports integration with a wide variety of messaging channels, including Microsoft Teams, Web Chat, Facebook Messenger, and others.

What Are Channels?

Channels are communication platforms that allow users to interact with your bot. By integrating your bot with multiple channels, you extend its reach to different audiences on various platforms.

Here are some of the most popular channels that Azure Bot Service supports:

1. **Microsoft Teams**:
   - Integrating your bot with **Microsoft Teams** allows users to interact with your bot within the Teams interface. Teams is widely used in corporate environments, and integrating your bot with it can streamline workflows and enhance collaboration.
   - To integrate with Teams, you need to configure your bot on the **Azure portal**, enable the Teams channel, and follow the necessary steps to authenticate and authorize your bot for Teams.
2. **Web Chat**:
   - Web Chat is the easiest channel to integrate if you have a website or web application. Azure Bot Service provides an embeddable Web Chat control that can be added to your website.
   - Once your bot is created in Azure, you can generate a Web Chat channel key, which allows you to embed the chatbot on your website.
3. **Facebook Messenger**:

- o Azure Bot Service can be integrated with **Facebook Messenger**, allowing users to interact with your bot on Facebook. This is useful for customer service bots or marketing campaigns where engagement through social media platforms is key.
- o You will need to create a **Facebook Developer account**, configure the Messenger settings, and authenticate the bot with Facebook's API.

4. **Other Channels**:
   - o Azure Bot Service supports integration with several other channels, including **Slack**, **Skype**, **Twilio SMS**, and **Direct Line** (for custom client applications). You can choose the channels that best suit your target audience and use case.

Steps to Integrate a Bot with Microsoft Teams:

1. In the **Azure portal**, navigate to your bot resource.
2. Under **Channels**, click **Microsoft Teams** and click **Save**.
3. Once the Teams channel is added, you will need to configure the bot's settings, including **authentication** and **permissions**.
4. Create a **Teams App** for your bot, and upload it to the Teams App Catalog.
5. After adding the bot to Teams, users will be able to interact with your bot within the Teams interface.

Testing the Bot on Multiple Channels:

- After configuring the channels, you can use the **Bot Framework Web Chat** or other channel simulators to test your bot across different platforms.
- Ensure that your bot's responses are appropriate for the specific channel. For example, a Facebook Messenger bot might need to handle images or quick replies, while a Teams bot may need to integrate with Teams-specific features like meetings or calendar events.

Understanding Dialogs and State Management

One of the most powerful features of Azure Bot Service is its ability to manage conversations using **dialogs** and **state management**. These features allow you to design complex conversational flows and maintain the state of the conversation across interactions.

Dialogs:

Dialogs are the building blocks of a conversation in Azure Bot Service. A dialog defines how the bot interacts with the user, guiding them through various steps based on their inputs.

1. **Simple Dialog**: A simple dialog prompts the user for information, waits for a response, and then processes that input. For example, a booking bot may ask, "What is your departure city?" and then process the user's input.

2. **Complex Dialogs**: Complex dialogs are used for multi-step interactions. They allow you to create workflows where the user needs to provide multiple pieces of information. For instance, in a flight booking application, the bot might need to collect the departure city, destination city, flight date, and passenger details.

Creating a Dialog in Azure Bot Service:

Dialogs can be created using the **Bot Framework SDK** or **Bot Framework Composer**. Here's an example of how to create a simple dialog in **C#**:

```csharp
Copy code
public class BookingDialog : ComponentDialog
```

```csharp
{
    public BookingDialog() : base(nameof(BookingDialog))
    {
        var waterfallSteps = new WaterfallStep[]
        {
            AskForDepartureCityAsync,
            AskForDestinationCityAsync,
            AskForFlightDateAsync,
            ConfirmBookingAsync
        };

        AddDialog(new WaterfallDialog(nameof(WaterfallDialog), waterfallSteps));
        AddDialog(new TextPrompt(nameof(TextPrompt)));
    }

    private async Task<DialogTurnResult>
AskForDepartureCityAsync(WaterfallStepContext stepContext, CancellationToken
cancellationToken)
    {
        return await stepContext.PromptAsync(nameof(TextPrompt), new
PromptOptions { Prompt = MessageFactory.Text("What is your departure city?") },
cancellationToken);
    }

    private async Task<DialogTurnResult>
AskForDestinationCityAsync(WaterfallStepContext stepContext, CancellationToken
cancellationToken)
    {
        var departureCity = (string)stepContext.Result;
```

```
        return await stepContext.PromptAsync(nameof(TextPrompt), new
PromptOptions { Prompt = MessageFactory.Text("What is your destination city?") },
cancellationToken);
    }


    private async Task<DialogTurnResult>
AskForFlightDateAsync(WaterfallStepContext stepContext, CancellationToken
cancellationToken)
    {
        return await stepContext.PromptAsync(nameof(TextPrompt), new
PromptOptions { Prompt = MessageFactory.Text("What is your desired flight
date?") }, cancellationToken);
    }


    private async Task<DialogTurnResult> ConfirmBookingAsync(WaterfallStepContext
stepContext, CancellationToken cancellationToken)
    {
        // Process the information and confirm the booking
        return await stepContext.EndDialogAsync(null, cancellationToken);
    }
}
```

This dialog walks the user through a series of steps to collect the information needed to make a flight booking.

State Management:

State management is essential to maintain context throughout the conversation. Azure Bot Service offers different types of state management, such as **User State** and **Conversation State**.

1. **User State**: Stores information about the user across multiple conversations. For example, storing a user's preferences or past bookings.
2. **Conversation State**: Stores data specific to a single conversation. This can include the user's current progress in a dialog or the responses they've provided so far.

Managing State:

Here's an example of how to implement state management in **C#**:

csharp
Copy code

```csharp
public class BookingBot : ActivityHandler
{
    private readonly IStatePropertyAccessor<BookingInfo> _bookingInfoAccessor;

    public BookingBot(UserState userState)
    {
        _bookingInfoAccessor = userState.CreateProperty<BookingInfo>("BookingInfo");
    }

    protected override async Task
OnMessageActivityAsync(ITurnContext<IMessageActivity> turnContext,
CancellationToken cancellationToken)
    {
        var bookingInfo = await _bookingInfoAccessor.GetAsync(turnContext, () => new
BookingInfo(), cancellationToken);

        // Update the booking information
        bookingInfo.LastMessage = turnContext.Activity.Text;
```

```
    await _bookingInfoAccessor.SetAsync(turnContext, bookingInfo,
cancellationToken);


    await turnContext.SendActivityAsync(MessageFactory.Text($"You said:
{turnContext.Activity.Text}"), cancellationToken);
    }
}
```

In this example, the **BookingInfo** class stores information such as the user's flight booking details, and the bot's conversation continues based on this data.

Conclusion

Azure Bot Service is a powerful and flexible platform for creating intelligent conversational agents. In this chapter, we covered the essential concepts for building and deploying a basic chatbot, integrating it with various messaging channels, and managing the flow of conversations using dialogs and state management. By using the tools and techniques provided by Azure Bot Service, you can create highly responsive, intelligent bots that engage users across a wide variety of platforms.

Chapter 8: Advanced Bot Framework Scenarios

In this chapter, we will explore advanced scenarios for working with Azure Bot Service and the Microsoft Bot Framework. These topics are crucial for creating bots that provide richer user interactions, ensure data security, and can be extended with additional functionalities via custom skills and APIs.

The chapter is divided into three primary sections:

1. **Implementing Adaptive Cards and Rich Responses**: Learn how to create and use Adaptive Cards to deliver visually rich responses to users.
2. **Securely Managing User Data in Bots**: Understand how to implement secure practices for handling user data within your bot applications.
3. **Extending Bots with Custom Skills and APIs**: Explore how to extend the functionality of your bots by integrating custom skills and APIs to provide more dynamic and context-aware responses.

By the end of this chapter, you will have the knowledge to create bots with visually appealing responses, manage user data securely, and add advanced capabilities to your bots using custom skills and APIs.

1. Implementing Adaptive Cards and Rich Responses

Adaptive Cards provide a way to create interactive, visually rich content in your bot responses. These cards can contain various elements such as images, buttons, text, and even input fields, all of which can be used to engage users more effectively.

What Are Adaptive Cards?

An **Adaptive Card** is a type of message format used to display interactive content within your bot's responses. Unlike traditional text-based responses, Adaptive Cards are flexible and can adapt their layout depending on the platform they are displayed on, such as Microsoft Teams, Outlook, or Web Chat. This enables bots to deliver a more dynamic, richer user experience.

Some key features of Adaptive Cards include:

- **Rich Layouts**: You can include images, buttons, input fields, and other interactive elements in the card.
- **Multi-Platform Support**: Adaptive Cards work seamlessly across various platforms like Teams, Web Chat, and Outlook.
- **Card Actions**: Cards can include actions, such as opening a webpage or submitting data, enabling users to interact with the bot in meaningful ways.

Creating Adaptive Cards

To create an Adaptive Card, you need to define its content using a **JSON** schema. Microsoft provides an **Adaptive Card Designer** tool that helps you visually design and generate the JSON code for your cards.

Example: Simple Adaptive Card

Here is an example of a simple Adaptive Card in JSON format:

json

Copy code

```json
{
  "$schema": "http://adaptivecards.io/schemas/adaptive-card.json",
  "type": "AdaptiveCard",
  "version": "1.2",
  "body": [
    {
      "type": "TextBlock",
      "text": "Welcome to the Chatbot!"
    },
    {
      "type": "TextBlock",
      "text": "How can I assist you today?"
    },
    {
      "type": "Input.Text",
      "id": "userQuery",
      "placeholder": "Type your question here"
    },
    {
      "type": "ActionSet",
      "actions": [
        {
          "type": "Action.Submit",
          "title": "Submit",
          "data": {
            "action": "submitQuery"
          }
        }
```

```
        }
      ]
    }
  ]
}
```

In this example, the card displays a welcome message, a text input field for the user to enter their query, and a submit button. Once the user submits the form, the bot can process the response and trigger an action.

Integrating Adaptive Cards in Your Bot

To use Adaptive Cards in a bot, you can create a message activity with the card as the content. Here's an example of how to send an Adaptive Card from a bot in **C#**:

```csharp
Copy code
var adaptiveCardJson = "<AdaptiveCard JSON string here>";
var adaptiveCardAttachment = new Attachment
{
    ContentType = "application/vnd.microsoft.card.adaptive",
    Content = JsonConvert.DeserializeObject(adaptiveCardJson)
};

var message = MessageFactory.Attachment(adaptiveCardAttachment);
await turnContext.SendActivityAsync(message, cancellationToken);
```

This code sends an Adaptive Card as part of the bot's response, allowing users to interact with it.

Handling User Interactions with Adaptive Cards

You can handle user interactions with Adaptive Cards by using **Action.Submit** elements. These actions submit data to the bot, allowing it to process the information and provide relevant responses.

Example of handling a button click in the bot:

csharp

Copy code

```csharp
if (turnContext.Activity.Value != null)
{
    var actionData = turnContext.Activity.Value as JObject;
    var actionType = actionData["action"]?.ToString();

    if (actionType == "submitQuery")
    {
        // Process the user's query
        var userQuery = actionData["userQuery"]?.ToString();
        await turnContext.SendActivityAsync($"You asked: {userQuery}",
cancellationToken);
    }
}
```

This code processes the form submission from the Adaptive Card and sends a confirmation message to the user.

---

2. Securely Managing User Data in Bots

Security and privacy are critical considerations when developing chatbots that handle sensitive user information. Azure Bot Service provides several tools and practices for securing user data and ensuring your bot complies with privacy regulations.

Best Practices for Managing User Data

When building bots, it's important to handle user data responsibly. Here are some key practices:

1. **Data Encryption**:
   - Always use **SSL/TLS encryption** to secure communication between the user and the bot. Azure Bot Service automatically encrypts communication with clients, but it's important to ensure that the data is securely transmitted between your bot and any external services it interacts with.
2. **Secure Storage**:
   - Avoid storing sensitive information like passwords or credit card details in bot memory. If necessary, use **Azure Key Vault** to securely store credentials and API keys.
   - For temporary state storage, use **Azure Cosmos DB** or **Azure Table Storage** with encrypted fields.
3. **User Authentication and Authorization**:
   - If your bot needs to access protected resources, implement authentication mechanisms such as **OAuth 2.0** or **Azure Active Directory (AAD)** to ensure that only authorized users can interact with the bot.
   - **Adaptive Cards** can also integrate with authentication services like **OAuth 2.0** to ensure secure interactions.
4. **Compliance with Regulations**:
   - Ensure that your bot complies with privacy regulations such as the **General Data Protection Regulation (GDPR)** or **Health Insurance Portability and Accountability Act (HIPAA)**. For example, your bot should be designed to handle data requests and deletions in a manner that complies with these regulations.

o Provide **data retention policies** for storing and deleting user data after a certain period of inactivity.

5. **Bot Auditing and Monitoring**:

o Use **Azure Monitor** and **Azure Application Insights** to track and log user interactions with your bot. This will help in identifying potential security threats and ensuring your bot adheres to privacy best practices.

o Implement logging for every action taken by the bot, including user input and actions that involve sensitive information.

Securing User Data with Azure Bot Service

Azure Bot Service provides features like **user authentication**, **secure storage**, and **role-based access control** (RBAC) to help ensure that sensitive data is handled securely. Additionally, you can leverage **Azure Active Directory** to manage user access to your bot services.

---

3. Extending Bots with Custom Skills and APIs

One of the most powerful features of the Azure Bot Framework is the ability to extend the capabilities of your bot through **custom skills** and **APIs**. Custom skills allow your bot to interact with external services, integrate with enterprise systems, or provide more advanced functionality to users.

What Are Custom Skills?

A **custom skill** is an extension of your bot's functionality that can be added through the Bot Framework Skill SDK. These skills can integrate with external systems, perform specific tasks, and provide dynamic responses based on data.

- **Order Management System**: A bot that checks inventory, places orders, and tracks shipments.
- **HR Services**: A bot that retrieves employee data, updates records, or manages payroll information.
- **Customer Support**: A bot that pulls data from CRM systems like **Salesforce** or **Microsoft Dynamics** to answer customer queries.

Building Custom Skills

Custom skills are developed by implementing a skill handler that processes user input and integrates with external services. You can build a custom skill using the **Bot Framework SDK** and then add it to your bot application.

Here's an example of how to create a simple custom skill in **C#**:

csharp

Copy code

```
public class OrderManagementSkill : SkillHandler
{
    public OrderManagementSkill(ConversationState conversationState, UserState userState)
        : base(conversationState, userState)
    {
    }

    protected override async Task<DialogTurnResult>
OnMessageActivityAsync(ITurnContext turnContext, CancellationToken cancellationToken)
    {
```

```csharp
        var orderId = turnContext.Activity.Text;
        var orderDetails = await GetOrderDetailsAsync(orderId);

        await turnContext.SendActivityAsync($"Order details: {orderDetails}",
cancellationToken);
        return await base.OnMessageActivityAsync(turnContext, cancellationToken);
    }


    private async Task<string> GetOrderDetailsAsync(string orderId)
    {
        // Call external system API to get order details
        return $"Details for order {orderId}: ...";
    }
}
```

This custom skill retrieves order details from an external system and returns them to the user.

Exposing APIs to Bot Framework

In addition to creating custom skills, you can also expose your bot to external services through **APIs**. This allows your bot to interact with databases, third-party services, or other microservices to fetch dynamic information and provide personalized experiences.

Example: Connecting to an API:

Here's how you can call an external API from your bot:

csharp

Copy code

```csharp
public async Task<string> GetWeatherAsync(string city)
```

```csharp
{
    var httpClient = new HttpClient();
    var response = await
httpClient.GetAsync($"https://api.weather.com/v3/weather/{city}");

    if (response.IsSuccessStatusCode)
    {
        var data = await response.Content.ReadAsStringAsync();
        return $"The current weather in {city} is: {data}";
    }
    else
    {
        return "Sorry, I couldn't retrieve the weather information at the moment.";
    }
}
```

In this example, the bot calls a weather API and returns the weather data to the user.

Conclusion

In this chapter, we covered several advanced scenarios for building and extending bots using the Microsoft Bot Framework. From creating visually rich responses using **Adaptive Cards** to managing sensitive data securely and extending bot functionality with **custom skills** and **APIs**, these features enable you to build sophisticated, enterprise-ready bots.

Chapter 9: Speech Recognition and Synthesis

In this chapter, we will delve into **Azure Speech Services**, focusing on two critical aspects: **speech recognition** and **speech synthesis**. These technologies are powerful tools for creating voice-enabled applications that can convert spoken language into text (Speech-to-Text or STT) and transform text into natural-sounding speech (Text-to-Speech or TTS). As part of **Azure Cognitive Services**, these capabilities enable developers to implement sophisticated voice interfaces across a wide range of devices and applications.

We will explore the following sections:

1. **Overview of Azure Speech Services**
2. **Real-Time Speech-to-Text Applications**
3. **Real-Time Text-to-Speech Applications**

---

1. Overview of Azure Speech Services

Azure Speech Services is a suite of cloud-based APIs provided by Microsoft to enable speech recognition, speech synthesis, speaker identification, and translation. These services are designed to help developers incorporate speech capabilities into their applications and products.

Key Features of Azure Speech Services

1. **Speech-to-Text (STT)**: This service converts spoken language into written text, enabling applications to transcribe conversations, commands, or audio recordings into text in real-time.
2. **Text-to-Speech (TTS)**: This service converts written text into lifelike speech, allowing applications to interact with users through voice.
3. **Speaker Recognition**: This technology allows applications to recognize and verify individual speakers based on their voice patterns.
4. **Speech Translation**: The service also provides real-time translation of spoken language, enabling multilingual conversations.
5. **Custom Speech**: You can build custom speech models to improve accuracy by training them on domain-specific data.

How Azure Speech Services Work

Azure Speech Services rely on advanced **machine learning** and **natural language processing** models that have been trained on massive datasets. These models are continually updated and optimized to recognize a wide range of accents, languages, and speech patterns.

The Speech SDK allows developers to integrate these capabilities into their applications. The SDK supports several programming languages, including **C#**, **Python**, **JavaScript**, and **Java**. The service also provides a REST API for HTTP-based interactions.

2. Real-Time Speech-to-Text Applications

Speech-to-Text technology, also known as **automatic speech recognition (ASR)**, converts audio input into written text. It plays a crucial role in a wide variety of applications such as voice assistants, transcription tools, and real-time communication platforms.

Real-Time Speech-to-Text Process

The real-time process of converting speech into text involves several stages:

1. **Audio Input**: The user speaks into a microphone or other input device.
2. **Speech Recognition**: The audio is sent to the Azure Speech Service, which processes the speech using machine learning models to transcribe it into text.
3. **Text Output**: The transcribed text is returned in real-time and can be used in applications such as voice commands, transcription services, or voice-based navigation.

Example: Real-Time Speech-to-Text in a C# Application

```csharp
Copy code
using Microsoft.CognitiveServices.Speech;
using System;
using System.Threading.Tasks;

public class SpeechToText
{
    public async Task TranscribeSpeechAsync()
    {
        var speechConfig = SpeechConfig.FromSubscription("YourSubscriptionKey", "YourRegion");
        var audioConfig = AudioConfig.FromDefaultMicrophoneInput();
```

```csharp
        var recognizer = new SpeechRecognizer(speechConfig, audioConfig);

        var result = await recognizer.RecognizeOnceAsync();

        if (result.Reason == ResultReason.RecognizedSpeech)
        {
            Console.WriteLine($"Recognized: {result.Text}");
        }
        else if (result.Reason == ResultReason.NoMatch)
        {
            Console.WriteLine("No speech could be recognized");
        }
        else if (result.Reason == ResultReason.Canceled)
        {
            var cancellationDetails = result.CancellationDetails;
            Console.WriteLine($"Speech Recognition canceled: {cancellationDetails.Reason}");
            Console.WriteLine($"Error details: {cancellationDetails.ErrorDetails}");
        }
    }
}
```

This code initializes a **SpeechRecognizer** object that listens for speech input from the microphone. The recognized text is then output to the console.

Use Cases for Real-Time Speech-to-Text

- **Transcription**: Converting meetings, lectures, or interviews into text format for accessibility, searchability, and record-keeping.

- **Voice Command Applications**: Enabling users to control devices or applications using spoken commands.
- **Interactive Voice Response (IVR)**: Automating customer service systems that respond to voice input.

3. Real-Time Text-to-Speech Applications

Text-to-Speech (TTS) technology, on the other hand, is used to convert written text into spoken language. With advancements in machine learning and neural network-based speech synthesis models, the quality of text-to-speech has significantly improved, allowing for more natural and expressive voice outputs.

Real-Time Text-to-Speech Process

The TTS process is as follows:

1. **Text Input**: The application provides written text to the speech service.
2. **Synthesis**: Azure Speech Service processes the text and converts it into audio using a neural text-to-speech model.
3. **Audio Output**: The synthesized speech is returned as an audio file or streamed in real-time to the user's device.

Example: Real-Time Text-to-Speech in a C# Application

```csharp
Copy code
using Microsoft.CognitiveServices.Speech;
using System;
using System.Threading.Tasks;

public class TextToSpeech
{
```

```csharp
public async Task ConvertTextToSpeechAsync(string text)
{
    var speechConfig = SpeechConfig.FromSubscription("YourSubscriptionKey", "YourRegion");

    var synthesizer = new SpeechSynthesizer(speechConfig);
    var result = await synthesizer.SpeakTextAsync(text);

    if (result.Reason == ResultReason.SynthesizingAudioCompleted)
    {
        Console.WriteLine($"Successfully synthesized the text: {text}");
    }
    else if (result.Reason == ResultReason.Canceled)
    {
        var cancellationDetails = result.CancellationDetails;
        Console.WriteLine($"Speech synthesis canceled: {cancellationDetails.Reason}");
        Console.WriteLine($"Error details: {cancellationDetails.ErrorDetails}");
    }
}
```

In this example, a **SpeechSynthesizer** object is used to convert the input text into speech and play it back to the user.

Use Cases for Real-Time Text-to-Speech

- **Virtual Assistants**: Providing spoken responses in voice-driven applications like Siri, Alexa, or Google Assistant.

- **Accessibility**: Enabling visually impaired users to interact with digital content through speech output.
- **Navigation Systems**: Giving real-time spoken directions in GPS or driving applications.

Chapter 10: Customizing Speech Models

In this chapter, we will focus on customizing speech models to improve the recognition and synthesis of speech for domain-specific or personalized applications. These customizations are essential for applications requiring high accuracy or specific use cases such as speaker identification, custom accents, or industry-specific jargon.

We will cover the following areas:

1. **Training Custom Speech Models**
2. **Working with Speaker Recognition and Verification**
3. **Deploying Speech Solutions at Scale**

---

1. Training Custom Speech Models

Custom Speech allows developers to enhance the accuracy of speech recognition models by training them with domain-specific data, specialized vocabulary, or custom accents. Training custom speech models is particularly useful when the standard models do not perform well in specific environments or with specialized terminology.

The Custom Speech Process

1. **Data Collection**: First, you need to collect a dataset that includes speech samples and corresponding text transcripts. This data should cover the terminology, accents, and other specific speech characteristics of your use case.

2. **Data Preparation**: Prepare the data by cleaning it and formatting it into an acceptable format for training, typically in WAV format for audio files and a text file for transcripts.

3. **Model Training**: Use Azure's **Custom Speech** service to train the model with your data. You can upload the data to the Azure portal and use it to train a model that adapts to your specific needs.

4. **Model Evaluation and Tuning**: After the model is trained, test its performance on new audio samples. Azure provides tools to evaluate the model's accuracy and make adjustments to improve its performance.

5. **Model Deployment**: Once you're satisfied with the model's accuracy, you can deploy it to Azure and integrate it into your applications.

Example: Training a Custom Speech Model

To train a custom speech model, you would need to use Azure's **Speech SDK** along with the **Custom Speech Portal**. The training process can be initiated from the portal, where you can upload your dataset and configure the model settings.

---

2. Working with Speaker Recognition and Verification

Speaker recognition and **verification** are advanced capabilities that go beyond speech recognition. These technologies identify and verify speakers based on their unique vocal characteristics, such as pitch, cadence, and tone.

Speaker Recognition vs. Speaker Verification

- **Speaker Recognition**: Identifies a speaker from a set of known voices (e.g., verifying a user in a voice-activated system).
- **Speaker Verification**: Confirms that the speaker is the person they claim to be (e.g., verifying the identity of a user accessing a secure system).

How Speaker Recognition Works

1. **Voice Enrollment**: The speaker provides samples of their voice, which are used to create a voice profile.
2. **Voice Comparison**: When the speaker speaks again, their voice is compared to the stored voice profile to verify or identify the speaker.

Use Cases for Speaker Recognition

- **Voice Biometrics**: Used in security systems for authenticating users.
- **Personalized Experiences**: Identifying speakers to provide tailored experiences, such as voice-activated assistants that recognize individual users.

---

3. Deploying Speech Solutions at Scale

Deploying speech solutions at scale involves managing large volumes of audio data, ensuring high availability, and ensuring the system performs efficiently under heavy loads.

Considerations for Scalability

1. **Distributed Architecture**: Use **Azure's cloud services** to scale speech recognition services across multiple regions to improve availability and reduce latency.

2. **Batch Processing**: For large-scale transcription needs (e.g., transcribing hundreds of hours of audio), batch processing can be used to process audio files in parallel, optimizing processing time.

3. **Cost Management**: Use **Azure Cost Management tools** to monitor the cost of running speech services at scale and optimize usage to prevent overspending.

Best Practices for Deployment

- Use **Azure Kubernetes Service (AKS)** for containerizing speech applications and scaling them based on demand.

- Implement **load balancing** and **caching** strategies to optimize response times and manage large numbers of concurrent users.

- Ensure that data privacy and compliance requirements (e.g., GDPR) are met when processing user audio data at scale.

Conclusion

In this chapter, we covered a range of advanced topics related to Azure Speech Services, from **speech recognition** and **synthesis** to the customization of speech models and working with speaker recognition technologies. Understanding how to train and deploy custom speech models and securely scale your speech solutions is crucial for building enterprise-level applications that offer voice-driven interfaces. With the capabilities offered by Azure, you can create powerful speech-enabled solutions that are accurate, scalable, and personalized for your user

Chapter 11: Integrating AI Solutions

In this chapter, we will explore how to **orchestrate AI workflows** and integrate multiple **Azure AI solutions** to create seamless, automated, and intelligent applications. The power of Azure lies not only in its standalone AI services but also in its ability to combine those services and integrate them into larger workflows. **Azure Logic Apps** and **Power Automate** play a pivotal role in this integration, providing low-code/no-code platforms for building automated workflows that incorporate AI solutions and other Azure services. Additionally, we will dive into how to monitor and log AI applications, ensuring they perform optimally in production.

We will cover the following sections:

1. **Leveraging Azure Logic Apps and Power Automate**
2. **Combining Multiple AI Services for End-to-End Scenarios**
3. **Monitoring and Logging AI Applications**

---

1. Leveraging Azure Logic Apps and Power Automate

Azure Logic Apps and **Power Automate** are two powerful tools for automating workflows in the Azure ecosystem. These services allow you to design, implement, and manage workflows that integrate multiple services and systems without needing extensive programming skills. Let's explore both services in detail.

Azure Logic Apps: An Overview

Azure Logic Apps is a cloud-based service that helps you build workflows that automate processes across a variety of applications and services. It supports a wide range of connectors for Azure services, SaaS applications (like Salesforce, Dynamics 365, and ServiceNow), and custom APIs. You can use Logic Apps to trigger workflows based on events and data, process that data, and interact with external systems.

Core Features of Logic Apps

- **Pre-built connectors**: Azure Logic Apps supports connectors for hundreds of popular services like Office 365, Dynamics 365, and Azure Cognitive Services.
- **Visual Workflow Design**: The Logic Apps Designer offers a visual interface for building workflows by simply dragging and dropping components, making it accessible even to users with limited coding experience.
- **Triggers and Actions**: Logic Apps workflows begin with a trigger (e.g., when a new email is received) and then perform actions (e.g., analyzing the email's sentiment using Text Analytics API).
- **Custom Workflow Logic**: You can create advanced workflows with conditions, loops, and other logic constructs.

Example Use Case for Azure Logic Apps

Imagine you are building a customer service automation system that integrates AI and other services. A typical workflow could look like this:

1. **Trigger**: When a new customer service email arrives in your Outlook inbox.

2. **Action 1**: The email is analyzed using the **Azure Text Analytics API** to extract key phrases and detect sentiment.
3. **Action 2**: Based on sentiment (positive, neutral, or negative), an appropriate response is drafted using **Azure OpenAI** or a similar service.
4. **Action 3**: The response is sent back to the customer via email.
5. **Action 4**: A log entry is created in **Azure Monitor** for auditing purposes.

This simple workflow can be achieved without writing extensive code, thanks to the integration of AI and cloud services in Logic Apps.

Power Automate: An Overview

Power Automate, previously known as Microsoft Flow, is a service that enables you to create automated workflows between applications and services. It's a similar platform to Azure Logic Apps but is designed with a more user-friendly interface for business users, enabling them to automate repetitive tasks and processes across a variety of applications.

Core Features of Power Automate

- **Pre-built Templates**: Power Automate provides hundreds of pre-built templates for common use cases, such as collecting email attachments or synchronizing data between apps.
- **Automating Tasks with Triggers**: Power Automate workflows are built around triggers and actions, such as "When a new file is created" or "When a tweet contains specific keywords."
- **Integration with Microsoft Power Platform**: Power Automate integrates seamlessly with other parts of the **Microsoft Power Platform**, including **Power BI** (for data visualization) and **PowerApps** (for building apps).

Power Automate can be used to automate repetitive tasks in an enterprise environment. For example:

1. **Trigger**: When a new file is uploaded to a SharePoint document library.
2. **Action 1**: Use the **Azure Cognitive Services** to analyze the content of the document using the **Text Analytics API** for sentiment and language detection.
3. **Action 2**: If the sentiment is negative, send an alert to the team via Microsoft Teams.
4. **Action 3**: Log the event to an **Azure SQL Database** for tracking.

This workflow can be built using the drag-and-drop interface without writing a single line of code, and can seamlessly integrate with various AI services and other Microsoft applications.

Benefits of Using Logic Apps and Power Automate

- **Low-Code Automation**: Both Logic Apps and Power Automate offer low-code platforms for automation, enabling business users, as well as developers, to create workflows.
- **AI Integration**: Both services offer deep integration with Azure AI services, enabling you to incorporate AI capabilities like sentiment analysis, computer vision, and speech recognition into workflows easily.
- **Enhanced Productivity**: By automating repetitive tasks, you can significantly reduce manual effort and improve efficiency.

---

2. Combining Multiple AI Services for End-to-End Scenarios

Integrating multiple AI services from **Azure Cognitive Services** allows you to create end-to-end intelligent workflows that can address more complex business challenges. By combining **computer vision**, **speech recognition**, **natural language processing (NLP)**, and **machine learning (ML)** models, you can create sophisticated solutions that automate and enhance business processes.

End-to-End Workflow Example: Intelligent Document Processing

One powerful example of combining multiple AI services is **intelligent document processing**. Here's how multiple services could be integrated to create an end-to-end solution:

1. **Input (Document Receipt)**: A document (e.g., invoice) is uploaded to a storage system like **Azure Blob Storage** or **SharePoint**.
2. **Optical Character Recognition (OCR)**: Use **Azure Computer Vision**'s **OCR API** to extract text from the image or PDF document.
3. **Text Analytics**: Once the text is extracted, the document's content is analyzed using **Azure Text Analytics** for sentiment analysis, key phrase extraction, and language detection.
4. **Entity Recognition**: Using **Azure Language Understanding (LUIS)**, you can identify entities like company names, invoice numbers, and total amounts.
5. **Data Classification**: Use **Azure Machine Learning** to classify the document type and route it to the appropriate workflow. For example, invoices could be sent to an approval queue, while customer feedback might be sent to a customer service team.
6. **Output (Action)**: Based on the classification, actions are triggered. For example, an email notification could be sent to the finance team, or the invoice could be approved automatically based on pre-defined rules.

Benefits of Combining Multiple AI Services

- **Automated Data Extraction and Classification**: Extracting data from documents and automatically classifying them saves time and reduces human error.
- **Smarter Business Workflows**: Using AI for document processing, customer feedback analysis, or product recommendations improves decision-making.
- **Scalability**: Azure's cloud-based services can easily scale to handle increasing workloads without requiring significant infrastructure investment.

---

3. Monitoring and Logging AI Applications

Once your AI solutions are up and running, it's essential to ensure they are performing as expected. **Monitoring and logging** are critical components of maintaining the health, performance, and security of your AI applications in production.

Azure Monitor and Azure Application Insights

Azure Monitor and **Azure Application Insights** are powerful tools for tracking the performance of your AI applications. They allow you to gather telemetry data, monitor application health, and troubleshoot any issues that arise.

Azure Monitor

Azure Monitor is a comprehensive solution for collecting, analyzing, and acting on telemetry data from your applications and services. It can be used to monitor the health of your AI models, track system performance, and set up alerts for potential issues.

Azure Application Insights

Application Insights provides deep diagnostics and performance insights for your web applications. It can track how users interact with your applications and detect anomalies in real-time. For AI solutions, this is helpful for detecting slow response times, issues in processing pipelines, and other potential bottlenecks.

Setting Up Monitoring for AI Workflows

1. **Data Collection**: Enable logging to collect telemetry data such as user interactions, model predictions, error logs, and response times.

2. **Metrics**: Set up **Azure Metrics** to track the performance of your services, including the number of requests to the AI model, response times, and error rates.

3. **Alerts**: Define **Azure Alerts** to automatically notify administrators when certain thresholds are breached (e.g., when the accuracy of an AI model falls below a predefined level).

4. **Dashboard**: Use **Azure Dashboards** to create customized views of your application's performance, including AI metrics.

Logging Best Practices

- **Log Every Action**: Ensure that each part of your AI workflow (e.g., data preprocessing, model inference) is logged to track performance and troubleshoot issues.

- **Use Structured Logging**: Structured logs make it easier to query and analyze logs, especially when dealing with large volumes of data.

- **Monitor Model Performance**: Keep an eye on how well your AI models are performing, checking for model drift or performance degradation over time.

Conclusion

In this chapter, we explored how to orchestrate AI workflows using **Azure Logic Apps** and **Power Automate**, combining multiple Azure AI services for end-to-end scenarios, and setting up monitoring and logging for AI applications. By leveraging these tools, you can create powerful, automated workflows that incorporate various AI capabilities and ensure that your AI applications are performing at their best. Whether you're automating business processes, integrating AI into larger systems, or ensuring your AI models are running smoothly, Azure provides the tools and services needed to build robust AI solutions.

Chapter 12: Scaling AI Solutions

As AI solutions grow in complexity and usage, the challenge of scaling them effectively arises. Scaling AI applications ensures that they can handle increased workloads, provide optimal performance, and do so while managing costs. The implementation of efficient AI models, choosing the right infrastructure for deployment, and managing resources effectively are key elements in achieving scalable AI solutions. In this chapter, we will explore strategies for scaling AI models, leveraging **Azure Kubernetes Service (AKS)** for efficient AI deployments, and understanding how to manage costs and resources in the cloud.

The primary topics of this chapter are:

1. **Optimizing AI Models for Performance**

2. **Using Azure Kubernetes Service (AKS) for AI Deployments**
3. **Managing Costs and Resources Effectively**

---

1. Optimizing AI Models for Performance

Before scaling your AI models across multiple instances or services, it is crucial to optimize their performance. Performance optimization helps ensure that your models run efficiently, reduce latency, and use computational resources in an optimal manner.

Key Areas for AI Model Optimization

1. **Model Compression and Pruning**
   - **Model Compression** involves reducing the size of the model without losing significant accuracy. Compression techniques like **quantization**, **weight pruning**, and **knowledge distillation** can make a model smaller and faster.
     - **Quantization**: This process converts floating-point weights into lower-precision representations (e.g., 8-bit integers). While this reduces the model's size, it can sometimes impact accuracy. However, recent advancements in quantization have significantly minimized the impact on model performance.
     - **Weight Pruning**: This technique removes certain weights (connections between neurons) that are considered redundant. By removing weights that have minimal impact on predictions, pruning results in a smaller, faster model.
     - **Knowledge Distillation**: This involves training a smaller model (student model) to replicate the behavior of a larger, more complex model (teacher model). The student model is faster and

more efficient, making it suitable for deployment on resource-constrained devices.

2. **Reducing Latency**

   o **Batching**: In many AI systems, requests can be batched together, reducing the need to process each request individually. Batching allows you to process several inputs simultaneously, improving throughput and reducing latency.

   o **Asynchronous Processing**: For systems that require real-time predictions but can tolerate some delay, **asynchronous processing** can be used. This allows for queuing requests and processing them in the background, freeing up resources for other tasks.

   o **Edge Computing**: By deploying AI models at the edge (on devices like IoT sensors or mobile phones), predictions can be made closer to the source of data, reducing the need for round-trip communication with a centralized cloud service. **Azure IoT Edge** is one such platform that allows the deployment of AI models to edge devices, enabling real-time processing with low latency.

3. **Parallelization and Distributed Computing**

   o **Distributed Training**: Training deep learning models often requires enormous computational resources, particularly for large datasets and complex models. Azure provides a **Distributed Training** framework, which allows splitting the training process across multiple nodes. This reduces the time needed to train large models and enables training with larger datasets.

   o **Parallel Inference**: Inference (or prediction) is the stage where AI models are used in real-world applications. To handle high throughput, parallel inference can be employed, where multiple instances of the model handle predictions in parallel.

4. **Optimizing Hyperparameters**

- Hyperparameter Tuning: Optimizing the hyperparameters of a model (such as learning rate, batch size, or the number of layers) is essential for improving performance. **Azure Machine Learning** offers **Hyperparameter Tuning** (also known as hyperparameter optimization), where various combinations of hyperparameters are tested to find the optimal configuration.
- AutoML: Azure's **AutoML** feature enables automatic selection of algorithms, hyperparameters, and feature engineering techniques. AutoML streamlines the model optimization process, making it easier to improve the performance of AI models.

Model Optimization Tools in Azure

- **Azure Machine Learning** provides several tools for model optimization, including automated hyperparameter tuning, distributed training, and pipeline orchestration.
- **Azure ML Managed Endpoints** allows you to deploy optimized models as endpoints for fast, scalable inference.
- **ONNX** (Open Neural Network Exchange) provides a cross-platform framework that supports optimizing AI models across different frameworks, ensuring compatibility and performance improvements during deployment.

---

2. Using Azure Kubernetes Service (AKS) for AI Deployments

When it comes to deploying AI models at scale, **Azure Kubernetes Service (AKS)** is one of the most efficient and effective solutions. AKS enables the deployment and orchestration of containerized AI applications, offering flexibility, scalability, and ease of management.

Introduction to Azure Kubernetes Service

Kubernetes is an open-source platform for automating the deployment, scaling, and management of containerized applications. **AKS** is Microsoft's managed Kubernetes service, which simplifies the process of deploying and managing applications using Kubernetes while taking care of infrastructure concerns such as scaling, patching, and monitoring.

With AKS, you can deploy machine learning models in containers, enabling easy scaling and management of AI workloads. Each container can host a different component of an AI solution, such as the model inference service, data processing, or pre-processing modules.

Benefits of Using AKS for AI Deployments

- **Scalability**: AKS allows you to easily scale your AI models horizontally (by adding more instances of a container) and vertically (by upgrading resources such as CPU and memory). This scalability is crucial for applications that experience fluctuating demands or need to scale out quickly.
- **High Availability**: Kubernetes ensures that your AI services are always available, distributing workloads across multiple nodes to maintain uptime and resilience even if individual instances fail.
- **Version Control**: Using containers ensures that your AI models are versioned and can be deployed in a consistent manner across different environments (development, testing, production). This helps maintain model integrity and reduces the risk of issues arising due to different configurations.

Deploying AI Models on AKS

1. **Containerization of AI Models**: Before deploying AI models on AKS, you need to containerize them. Docker is commonly used for containerization. The model, along with its dependencies, is packaged into a container image.

- o **Dockerfile**: A **Dockerfile** specifies the instructions to build the container image, including the AI model, its environment, and dependencies.
- o **Container Registry**: Once the image is built, it is pushed to a **container registry** (like Azure Container Registry), where it can be accessed by AKS.

2. **Setting Up the AKS Cluster**: AKS clusters are set up with various nodes that host containers. You can configure the cluster to auto-scale based on demand or set up custom rules to control how resources are allocated across containers.

3. **Deploying the Model to AKS**: Once the model is containerized and the AKS cluster is ready, you can deploy your AI model using **Kubernetes Deployments**. A Kubernetes **Deployment** defines the desired state for the application, ensuring that the specified number of replicas (container instances) is maintained.

4. **Scaling the Model**: AKS allows you to scale your model by adjusting the number of replicas or pods, either manually or automatically, based on predefined metrics such as CPU or memory usage.

5. **Monitoring and Management**: AKS integrates with **Azure Monitor** and **Azure Log Analytics** to track the health and performance of your deployed models. This provides insights into resource consumption, container health, and other critical metrics that help you maintain efficient operations.

Key AKS Features for AI Solutions

- **Autoscaling**: Both the **Horizontal Pod Autoscaler** and **Cluster Autoscaler** ensure that AI services scale automatically in response to traffic demands, maintaining optimal performance.

- **Load Balancing**: AKS provides integrated **load balancing** to distribute requests evenly across all container instances, ensuring high availability and reducing the risk of performance bottlenecks.

- **Security**: AKS integrates with **Azure Active Directory** and **Azure Key Vault**, enabling secure management of credentials and user access to sensitive data.

---

3. Managing Costs and Resources Effectively

As AI solutions scale, managing costs and resources efficiently becomes a critical task. Azure offers several tools and best practices that help you optimize resource usage and reduce unnecessary costs while maintaining performance.

Cost Management in Azure

Azure provides the **Azure Cost Management + Billing** tool to monitor and optimize the cost of resources. You can set budgets, view cost analysis, and identify areas where resources are being underutilized or overprovisioned.

Best Practices for Managing Costs

1. **Right-Sizing**: Ensure that your resources are appropriately sized for the tasks they are performing. Over-provisioning resources (e.g., CPUs, memory) increases costs without improving performance. Azure offers tools like **Azure Advisor** to recommend cost-saving optimizations based on your current resource usage.

2. **Azure Reservations**: For long-term projects, **Azure Reservations** allow you to pre-purchase Azure resources (like VMs or storage) at a discounted rate. This can result in significant savings if your workloads are predictable and require consistent resource allocation.

3. **Auto-Scaling**: Implement **auto-scaling** for your resources, such as AKS, to ensure that you only use resources when needed. By scaling your resources based on demand, you can prevent over-spending during periods of low usage.

4. **Monitoring Resource Utilization**: Use **Azure Monitor** to keep track of resource utilization and ensure that you are not over-allocating resources. You can set up alerts when resource usage goes beyond specified thresholds, allowing you to take action before incurring excessive costs.

5. **Spot Virtual Machines**: For non-critical AI workloads, consider using **Azure Spot Virtual Machines**. These VMs offer significant cost savings but can be evicted at any time. This is ideal for batch processing or other non-time-sensitive AI tasks.

Conclusion

In this chapter, we explored the essential strategies for scaling AI solutions, focusing on optimizing AI models for performance, deploying AI models using **Azure Kubernetes Service (AKS)**, and effectively managing costs and resources. As AI applications grow and evolve, the ability to scale them while maintaining optimal performance and managing costs will be crucial for their success. With the tools and services provided by Azure, organizations can build, deploy, and manage scalable AI solutions that meet their evolving needs, providing a strong foundation for future growth and innovation.

Chapter 13: Securing AI Solutions

As organizations increasingly leverage AI solutions, the importance of securing these systems becomes paramount. Ensuring that AI solutions are robust against threats, properly authenticated, and compliant with regulatory requirements is a critical part of the deployment lifecycle. Security, particularly when sensitive data is involved, must be designed into the AI infrastructure from the ground up.

In this chapter, we'll cover security best practices for implementing and managing AI solutions on Microsoft Azure. We will focus on strategies for **Role-Based Access Control (RBAC)** and securing sensitive data through **Azure Key Vault**.

---

1. Implementing Role-Based Access Control (RBAC)

Role-Based Access Control (RBAC) is a fundamental security feature in Azure, enabling organizations to enforce security policies by assigning permissions to users based on their roles. Implementing RBAC in AI solutions ensures that only authorized individuals and services can access specific resources and perform particular actions, minimizing the risk of unauthorized access or data breaches.

What is RBAC?

RBAC is an access control method used to define and enforce security policies by categorizing users into roles. Each role has specific permissions that dictate what actions a user or service can take on a given resource. Azure RBAC allows you to:

- **Grant permissions** based on roles to ensure that users only have access to the resources they need.
- **Enforce least-privilege access**, which reduces the attack surface of your applications by ensuring users and services have only the permissions necessary to complete their tasks.

In the context of AI solutions, RBAC can be applied to restrict access to AI models, datasets, and services like **Azure Machine Learning** or **Azure Cognitive Services**, where different users might need different levels of access.

Key Components of RBAC

1. **Roles**: A role defines the permissions that a user or service has. Azure comes with several built-in roles such as:
    - **Owner**: Full control over resources.
    - **Contributor**: Can create and manage resources, but cannot assign roles.
    - **Reader**: Can view resources but cannot modify them.
    - **Custom Roles**: Azure allows you to create custom roles tailored to your organization's needs.

2. **Assignments**: An assignment links a user or service to a specific role at a certain scope (such as a subscription, resource group, or specific resource).

3. **Scopes**: The scope defines the set of resources that a role applies to. For example:
    - **Subscription**: The user has access to all resources within the subscription.
    - **Resource Group**: Access is restricted to a specific set of resources.
    - **Resource**: Access can be limited to individual resources, such as an AI model or dataset.

How to Implement RBAC for AI Solutions

1. **Determine Roles and Permissions**: Before implementing RBAC, carefully assess the various types of users and services that will interact with your AI solutions. For instance, data scientists may require contributor-level access to **Azure Machine Learning** workspaces, while business analysts may only need reader access to the results of model predictions.

2. **Use Built-in Roles**: Azure offers built-in roles tailored to machine learning and AI workloads. For example:
    - **Machine Learning Contributor**: Grants permissions to manage machine learning experiments, models, and endpoints.

- o **Cognitive Services Contributor**: Allows users to manage Cognitive Services resources such as the **Azure Computer Vision** API, **Text Analytics**, and others.

3. **Apply RBAC at the Correct Scope**: Use Azure's RBAC capabilities to apply access control at the appropriate level (subscription, resource group, or resource). This granularity helps ensure that permissions are assigned based on the principle of least privilege.

4. **Review and Audit Permissions Regularly**: Once RBAC has been configured, regularly audit roles and permissions to ensure that users and services have appropriate access. Azure provides detailed audit logs that track who accessed what resources and when.

5. **Automate Role Assignments**: Use **Azure Active Directory (AAD)** and **Azure Policy** to automate role assignments based on organizational requirements. This can help maintain a consistent security posture across all AI projects and ensure that users and services are always assigned the appropriate access levels.

---

2. Managing Azure Key Vault for Sensitive Data

When working with AI solutions, it is common to deal with sensitive data such as authentication keys, connection strings, and personal information. Storing this data securely is essential to maintaining both the integrity and confidentiality of your solutions. **Azure Key Vault** provides a secure and centralized way to store and manage sensitive data used by AI models and applications.

What is Azure Key Vault?

Azure Key Vault is a cloud service that allows you to securely store and manage sensitive information like:

- **Secrets**: Data such as API keys, passwords, or connection strings.
- **Certificates**: SSL/TLS certificates or public/private key pairs used for encryption.
- **Keys**: Cryptographic keys used for encryption, decryption, or signing.

By using Azure Key Vault, organizations can enforce security best practices such as **centralized management**, **automated key rotation**, and **access control**.

How to Use Azure Key Vault for Securing AI Solutions

1. **Storing Secrets for AI Applications** AI models and applications often need access to credentials to connect to various services, such as databases, APIs, or third-party services. These credentials should never be hardcoded into your AI applications or stored in unencrypted files.
   - **Store API Keys**: Use Azure Key Vault to securely store API keys for accessing AI services, such as Azure Cognitive Services.
   - **Store Connection Strings**: If your AI solution interacts with databases or cloud storage, store connection strings in Key Vault to ensure they are not exposed in source code or configuration files.
2. **Encrypting Sensitive Data with Key Vault** AI solutions that handle sensitive data such as personally identifiable information (PII) must ensure that the data is encrypted both in transit and at rest. Azure Key Vault enables the use of **Azure Managed HSM** (Hardware Security Module) to generate, store, and manage encryption keys for your applications.
   - **Client-Side Encryption**: Before data is uploaded to cloud services, it can be encrypted using keys stored in Key Vault.
   - **Data Encryption for Model Training**: When training AI models with sensitive data, ensure that the data is encrypted during both the training and inference phases. Key Vault simplifies key management, making it easier to maintain encrypted datasets.

3. **Access Policies and Key Rotation** One of the major advantages of using Azure Key Vault is the ability to control who can access specific secrets, certificates, and keys.

   ○ **Access Policies**: Set granular access policies for different Azure Active Directory (AAD) users and service principals. For example, a data scientist might have read access to API keys for training an AI model but should not have write access to the secrets.

   ○ **Key Rotation**: Azure Key Vault supports automated key rotation, ensuring that secrets and keys are rotated regularly for enhanced security.

4. **Integrating Key Vault with AI Models** AI models often require access to various secrets for their operation, such as credentials for data storage or authentication for external services. Key Vault can be integrated into AI solutions using the **Azure SDKs** and APIs, ensuring that AI applications always access sensitive data securely.

   ○ **Service Principal Authentication**: Use service principals in Azure Active Directory to authenticate your AI application with Azure Key Vault. This ensures that only authorized applications can access secrets stored in Key Vault.

   ○ **Using Key Vault in Azure Machine Learning**: Azure Machine Learning integrates with Key Vault, allowing you to securely store and manage secrets like database credentials or API keys that your AI models might use.

Securing AI solutions is an essential part of developing and deploying robust, compliant, and scalable systems. In this chapter, we discussed the two main areas for securing AI solutions on Azure: **Role-Based Access Control (RBAC)** and **Azure Key Vault**.

RBAC helps to enforce the principle of least privilege by assigning roles with specific permissions to users and services, ensuring that only authorized parties can access and modify AI resources. Additionally, **Azure Key Vault** provides a secure and centralized solution for managing sensitive data such as credentials, encryption keys, and API keys, ensuring that AI solutions remain secure and compliant.

Chapter 14: Compliance and Responsible AI

In addition to securing AI solutions, it is essential to ensure that these systems adhere to industry standards, legal frameworks, and ethical guidelines. **Compliance** ensures that AI solutions operate within the boundaries of regulations, while **Responsible AI** frameworks help ensure that AI technologies are developed and deployed in an ethical and transparent manner.

In this chapter, we will discuss **compliance** requirements for AI solutions and explore **Microsoft's Responsible AI Framework** to ensure that AI systems are developed and deployed in a manner that aligns with ethical principles.

---

1. Ensuring Compliance with Industry Standards

As AI technologies evolve, various regulatory bodies and standards organizations have put in place frameworks to govern the ethical use of AI, ensuring that these technologies do not pose risks to individuals or society. Ensuring compliance with these standards is vital for organizations to avoid legal and reputational damage.

1. **General Data Protection Regulation (GDPR)**: The **GDPR** is one of the most comprehensive data protection laws globally and has significant implications for AI solutions that handle personal data.
   - AI systems must ensure that data is processed lawfully, transparently, and for specified purposes.
   - GDPR mandates **data minimization**, ensuring that only the necessary data is collected.
   - **Automated Decision-Making**: GDPR provides specific rules around the use of AI in automated decision-making, including the requirement for human oversight in significant decisions that impact individuals.

2. **Health Insurance Portability and Accountability Act (HIPAA)**: For AI solutions in healthcare, **HIPAA** regulations ensure that AI systems are compliant with the standards for protecting personal health information (PHI). AI applications must handle data securely and maintain confidentiality throughout processing and storage.

3. **Federal Trade Commission (FTC) Guidelines**: The **FTC** regulates the use of AI in consumer products, ensuring that AI technologies are used in a fair, transparent, and non-deceptive manner. The FTC focuses on preventing AI technologies from being used to mislead or exploit consumers.

4. **ISO/IEC Standards**: Several international standards such as **ISO/IEC 27001** (information security management) and **ISO/IEC 23894** (AI ethics) provide frameworks for ensuring that AI solutions are compliant with best practices for security, ethics, and transparency.

Ensuring Compliance in AI Development

- **Data Governance**: Ensure that data collection, processing, and storage comply with legal frameworks like GDPR, HIPAA, and others.

- **Model Transparency**: Make the AI model's decision-making process transparent and auditable. This can be achieved through explainable AI (XAI) techniques, where the model's predictions can be interpreted and understood by humans.
- **Auditing**: Regular audits of AI models and their processes help maintain compliance with industry standards.

---

2. Applying Microsoft's Responsible AI Framework

Microsoft's **Responsible AI Framework** is a set of guidelines and principles designed to help organizations develop AI solutions that are ethical, transparent, and aligned with societal values. It provides a framework for ensuring that AI models are fair, accountable, transparent, and explainable.

Key Principles of Responsible AI

1. **Fairness**: AI models should be trained on diverse datasets to ensure that the model's predictions are fair and unbiased. Microsoft's Responsible AI principles advocate for continuous monitoring of AI models to ensure that they do not propagate or amplify biases.
2. **Accountability**: Organizations should take responsibility for the outcomes of their AI models. This includes ensuring that models are tested for fairness and accuracy before deployment and taking steps to mitigate potential risks.
3. **Transparency**: AI models should be explainable. End users should be able to understand why certain predictions or decisions were made by the model, particularly in high-stakes applications like healthcare or finance.
4. **Privacy**: AI systems must respect user privacy. Personal data should only be collected when necessary and used responsibly, and users must have control over their data.

5. **Security**: AI solutions should be secure from malicious attacks. This includes using proper encryption methods, securing APIs, and following security best practices for data storage and transmission.
6. **Collaboration**: Microsoft encourages collaboration across industries to develop best practices for Responsible AI. By sharing knowledge and improving processes collectively, organizations can create better and more ethical AI technologies.

Conclusion

In this chapter, we explored two critical aspects of AI deployment: **Compliance** and **Responsible AI**. Ensuring that AI solutions adhere to industry standards, legal regulations, and ethical frameworks is essential to mitigate risks and maintain public trust.

By applying **Microsoft's Responsible AI Framework**, organizations can develop AI systems that are ethical, transparent, and aligned with societal values. Furthermore, maintaining compliance with regulations like **GDPR**, **HIPAA**, and **ISO standards** ensures that AI solutions are not only effective but also secure, fair, and accountable.

Adopting these principles will help organizations ensure that their AI solutions are developed responsibly, fostering trust and promoting the widespread adoption of AI technologies.

Chapter 15: Real-World Use Cases

Artificial Intelligence (AI) has rapidly evolved to become an integral part of industries across the globe. From enhancing customer experience to automating critical processes, AI is now a cornerstone of technological innovation. In this chapter, we will explore several real-world use cases where Microsoft Azure AI solutions are implemented to drive growth, efficiency, and innovation in diverse industries such as **Retail**, **E-Commerce**, **Healthcare**, and **Finance**. By understanding how AI is applied in these sectors, you can gain insight into the various ways Azure AI services can be leveraged to solve complex problems and enhance business operations.

---

1. AI in Retail and E-Commerce

The retail and e-commerce industries have seen some of the most transformative applications of AI. Whether it's creating personalized shopping experiences, optimizing inventory management, or predicting consumer demand, AI has fundamentally changed how businesses operate in this sector.

Personalized Customer Experiences

One of the most impactful ways AI is used in retail and e-commerce is to **personalize the shopping experience**. Using Azure AI's **Personalizer** and **Azure Cognitive Services**, businesses can analyze customer data to deliver targeted recommendations, content, and promotions that align with each shopper's preferences. This personalization is driven by machine learning algorithms that learn from consumer behaviors and preferences in real-time.

- **Example**: An online retailer uses AI to analyze browsing patterns, purchase history, and demographic data to recommend products that are most likely to interest a customer. Personalized recommendations lead to higher conversion rates and increased customer satisfaction.
- **Technology Used**: **Azure Personalizer, Azure Machine Learning, Azure Cognitive Services** (Text Analytics, Vision)

Customer Support Automation

AI-driven chatbots and virtual assistants are revolutionizing customer service in retail and e-commerce. These bots, built on **Azure Bot Services**, can interact with customers in natural language, answering queries, processing orders, and resolving issues 24/7. By utilizing natural language processing (NLP), the bots understand customer requests and provide relevant responses in a conversational manner.

- **Example**: A fashion retailer deploys a chatbot on their website and mobile app that assists customers in finding the right size, recommends outfits based on previous purchases, and helps with order tracking.
- **Technology Used**: **Azure Bot Services, Azure Cognitive Services (LUIS - Language Understanding)**

Demand Forecasting and Inventory Management

AI models can be trained to forecast demand based on historical sales data, seasonality, and market trends. By leveraging **Azure Machine Learning**, retailers can predict which products are likely to be in high demand, optimize their inventory, and ensure that stock levels are aligned with consumer preferences.

- **Example**: A grocery chain uses AI to predict demand for products based on factors like weather patterns, holidays, and local events. This helps them optimize supply chain logistics and minimize overstocking or stockouts.
- **Technology Used**: Azure Machine Learning, Azure Databricks, Azure Synapse Analytics

Visual Search and Image Recognition

Azure's **Computer Vision** services allow retailers to implement **visual search** capabilities. Customers can take photos of products and search for similar items in an online store. This technology leverages deep learning to identify patterns in images and match them with product catalogs.

- **Example**: A furniture retailer allows customers to upload images of furniture they like, and AI-powered search returns visually similar items from the store's catalog.
- **Technology Used**: Azure Computer Vision, Azure Custom Vision

Fraud Detection and Prevention

Retailers and e-commerce businesses are increasingly using AI to detect and prevent fraudulent activities, such as payment fraud and account takeovers. AI models analyze transaction patterns to identify anomalies that may indicate fraudulent activity.

- **Example**: An online retailer uses AI to monitor transaction data in real-time and flag suspicious activity, such as multiple purchases from different locations within a short period.
- **Technology Used**: Azure Machine Learning, Azure Cognitive Services (Anomaly Detector)

2. AI in Healthcare and Finance

AI in the healthcare and finance industries has led to significant advancements, including predictive analytics, automated decision-making, and enhanced patient care. Microsoft Azure provides a comprehensive suite of tools that help organizations in these sectors make data-driven decisions while ensuring compliance and security.

AI in Healthcare

Healthcare organizations are increasingly adopting AI to improve patient care, reduce operational costs, and enhance diagnostic accuracy. Azure AI offers a wide range of services to support these applications.

Predictive Analytics for Patient Outcomes

AI-driven predictive models can analyze historical patient data to predict future health outcomes, helping doctors make more informed decisions. For instance, AI can predict the likelihood of a patient developing chronic conditions like diabetes or cardiovascular diseases, allowing for earlier interventions and personalized treatment plans.

- **Example**: A hospital uses AI to predict the risk of patients developing sepsis based on vital signs, lab results, and medical history. Early detection helps healthcare providers intervene more quickly, reducing mortality rates.
- **Technology Used**: **Azure Machine Learning, Azure Synapse Analytics**

Medical Imaging and Diagnostics

Azure's **Computer Vision** and **Custom Vision** services have been particularly useful in analyzing medical images such as X-rays, MRIs, and CT scans. These AI models can detect abnormalities such as tumors or fractures, providing doctors with more accurate insights and reducing human error.

- **Example**: An oncology clinic uses AI to analyze mammograms and CT scans to detect early signs of breast cancer. The system can highlight potential issues for further investigation, speeding up the diagnostic process.
- **Technology Used**: **Azure Computer Vision**, **Azure Custom Vision**, **Azure Machine Learning**

Natural Language Processing for EHR (Electronic Health Records)

AI models can process unstructured data from Electronic Health Records (EHR) and extract meaningful insights. For example, **Text Analytics** can extract key medical conditions, medications, and allergies from clinical notes, providing healthcare professionals with a comprehensive view of a patient's health.

- **Example**: A healthcare provider uses **Azure Text Analytics** to scan doctor's notes and medical records, extracting key information to help physicians quickly understand a patient's medical history.
- **Technology Used**: **Azure Text Analytics**, **Azure Cognitive Search**

AI-Powered Virtual Health Assistants

Virtual assistants are transforming patient engagement in healthcare. Using **Azure Bot Services**, healthcare providers can deploy AI-powered assistants to provide patients with medical information, appointment scheduling, and even prescription refills.

- **Example**: A healthcare organization deploys a chatbot to answer patient queries, provide health information, and help schedule appointments with healthcare professionals.
- **Technology Used**: **Azure Bot Services**, **Azure Cognitive Services (LUIS)**

AI in Finance

The financial services industry is leveraging AI for everything from risk management to fraud detection. Azure AI tools provide banks, insurance companies, and investment firms with advanced capabilities to analyze financial data and improve customer experiences.

Fraud Detection and Risk Management

AI models can be used to analyze transaction data, identify patterns, and flag potential fraudulent activities. Azure's **Anomaly Detector** can be used to monitor financial transactions in real-time, helping financial institutions identify abnormal patterns that could indicate fraud.

- **Example**: A bank uses AI to monitor credit card transactions and flag potential fraud. The AI model analyzes factors like transaction size, location, and merchant type to detect anomalies.
- **Technology Used**: **Azure Anomaly Detector, Azure Machine Learning**

Algorithmic Trading and Investment Management

AI is also transforming the world of investment management. Azure's **Machine Learning** capabilities enable financial institutions to build predictive models for stock price forecasting and portfolio optimization. These models can analyze historical data, market trends, and news sentiment to identify profitable trading opportunities.

- **Example**: An investment firm uses AI to predict stock prices based on historical data and news sentiment analysis. The firm uses these predictions to optimize its trading strategies.
- **Technology Used**: **Azure Machine Learning, Azure Cognitive Services (Text Analytics)**

Customer Support and Chatbots

As with retail and e-commerce, financial institutions are using AI-powered chatbots to handle customer service inquiries, process transactions, and provide financial advice. **Azure Bot Services** allows organizations to build scalable and secure chatbot solutions.

- **Example**: A bank uses an AI-powered chatbot to assist customers with account balance inquiries, recent transactions, and even basic financial advice.
- **Technology Used**: Azure Bot Services, Azure Cognitive Services (LUIS)

Compliance and Regulatory Reporting

Financial institutions are also leveraging AI to ensure compliance with regulations like **Anti-Money Laundering (AML)** and **Know Your Customer (KYC)**. AI models can analyze transaction data and flag suspicious activity that may indicate money laundering or identity theft.

- **Example**: A financial institution uses AI to monitor customer transactions and flag suspicious activities that could indicate potential money laundering, helping to ensure compliance with regulatory standards.
- **Technology Used**: Azure Machine Learning, Azure Cognitive Services

---

Conclusion

AI is making a significant impact on industries such as **Retail**, **E-Commerce**, **Healthcare**, and **Finance**. Azure AI provides a robust set of tools that enable businesses to enhance customer experiences, streamline operations, and drive innovation. From predictive analytics and demand forecasting to fraud detection and customer support, AI-powered solutions are revolutionizing how companies across different sectors operate.

MCQs for AI-102: Designing and Implementing a Microsoft Azure AI Solution

1. **What is the primary purpose of Azure Cognitive Services?**
   - A) To provide advanced machine learning capabilities for big data
   - B) To allow easy integration of AI functionalities into applications without requiring deep machine learning knowledge
   - C) To store large datasets for machine learning applications
   - D) To provide hardware resources for training AI models
   - **Answer**: B

2. **Which Azure service can be used to train and deploy machine learning models?**
   - A) Azure Functions
   - B) Azure Machine Learning
   - C) Azure Logic Apps
   - D) Azure Cognitive Search
   - **Answer**: B

3. **Which Azure service is specifically designed for vision-related tasks such as image recognition and object detection?**
   - A) Azure Bot Service
   - B) Azure Cognitive Services – Computer Vision
   - C) Azure Machine Learning
   - D) Azure Speech Services
   - **Answer**: B

4. **Which of the following is NOT a service provided by Azure Cognitive Services?**
   - A) Vision
   - B) Language
   - C) Speech
   - D) Data Storage
   - **Answer**: D

5. **In Azure AI, what does LUIS stand for?**
   - A) Language Understanding Intelligent Service
   - B) Learning Unified Interface Service
   - C) Logical Unit Information Service
   - D) Latent Understanding and Intelligence System
   - **Answer**: A

6. **Which tool is best suited for building, training, and deploying custom AI models in Azure?**
   - A) Azure Bot Services
   - B) Azure Machine Learning
   - C) Azure Cognitive Services
   - D) Azure Functions
   - **Answer**: B

7. **What is the purpose of the Azure Personalizer service?**

- o A) To personalize customer interactions by analyzing behaviors and preferences
- o B) To analyze text data for sentiment analysis
- o C) To enhance visual search capabilities
- o D) To automate the deployment of machine learning models
- o **Answer**: A

8. **Which of the following services is used to create conversational AI bots in Azure?**
   - o A) Azure Bot Services
   - o B) Azure Functions
   - o C) Azure Logic Apps
   - o D) Azure Cognitive Services
   - o **Answer**: A

9. **What type of model does Azure Custom Vision use to classify images?**
   - o A) Pre-trained models only
   - o B) Custom-built models that are trained using your own image data
   - o C) Decision trees
   - o D) Artificial neural networks exclusively
   - o **Answer**: B

10. **Which Azure service provides the ability to translate text in multiple languages in real-time?**
    - o A) Azure Translator
    - o B) Azure Text Analytics
    - o C) Azure Speech Services
    - o D) Azure Machine Learning
    - o **Answer**: A

11. **Which of the following is the best approach for scaling an AI solution in Azure?**
    - o A) Using Azure Virtual Machines

- o B) Using Azure Kubernetes Service (AKS)

- o C) Using Azure Logic Apps

- o D) Using Azure Cognitive Services exclusively

- o **Answer**: B

12. **What type of AI applications can benefit from using Azure's Speech-to-Text service?**

- o A) Automated call centers

- o B) Image classification systems

- o C) Chatbots

- o D) Predictive analytics

- o **Answer**: A

13. **In Azure, which service would you use to build an AI-powered app that can recognize spoken commands?**

- o A) Azure Cognitive Services - Speech

- o B) Azure Machine Learning

- o C) Azure Bot Services

- o D) Azure Databricks

- o **Answer**: A

14. **What is Azure Logic Apps used for in AI-based workflows?**

- o A) To train machine learning models

- o B) To automate workflows and integrate various services, including AI

- o C) To perform speech recognition

- o D) To manage virtual machine resources

- o **Answer**: B

15. **Which feature of Azure Bot Services enables bots to understand user input more effectively?**

- o A) LUIS (Language Understanding)

- o B) Custom Vision

- o C) Azure Cognitive Search

- D) Azure Data Factory
- **Answer**: A

16. **What is the role of Azure Key Vault in an AI solution?**
    - A) It stores machine learning models.
    - B) It stores and manages secrets, such as API keys and passwords.
    - C) It hosts AI services like Cognitive Services.
    - D) It integrates AI workloads with other cloud services.
    - **Answer**: B

17. **What is the main purpose of the Azure Anomaly Detector?**
    - A) To detect outliers or anomalies in data that may indicate unusual behavior or fraud
    - B) To improve the performance of deep learning models
    - C) To classify images based on labeled data
    - D) To recognize speech patterns in text
    - **Answer**: A

18. **Which of the following is an example of a Natural Language Processing (NLP) task?**
    - A) Image classification
    - B) Sentiment analysis of text
    - C) Speech-to-text conversion
    - D) Object detection in images
    - **Answer**: B

19. **What is the key advantage of using Azure Kubernetes Service (AKS) for deploying AI solutions?**
    - A) AKS allows you to automatically scale AI models based on traffic
    - B) AKS provides a graphical interface for model development
    - C) AKS eliminates the need for data preprocessing
    - D) AKS provides pre-built machine learning models for easy deployment

- o **Answer**: A

20. **Which service would you use in Azure to process images and extract handwritten or printed text?**

    - o A) Azure Speech Services
    - o B) Azure Computer Vision
    - o C) Azure Translator
    - o D) Azure Bot Services
    - o **Answer**: B

21. **What is the main purpose of Azure Cognitive Search?**

    - A) To build and deploy machine learning models
    - B) To manage and scale AI applications
    - C) To enable powerful search capabilities over large datasets
    - D) To create conversational bots
    - **Answer**: C

22. **Which of the following services is best suited for identifying faces in images?**

    - A) Azure Cognitive Services – Face API
    - B) Azure Computer Vision
    - C) Azure Translator
    - D) Azure Machine Learning
    - **Answer**: A

23. **In the context of Azure, what does the acronym "NLP" stand for?**

    - A) Neural Learning Processing
    - B) Natural Language Processing
    - C) Network Level Protection
    - D) Nonlinear Pattern Learning
    - **Answer**: B

24. **What does Azure's Text Analytics API do?**

- A) Analyzes images for facial recognition
- B) Detects and classifies sentiment and key phrases from text
- C) Translates text into multiple languages
- D) Transforms text into speech
- **Answer**: B

25. **Which service in Azure is used for performing real-time speech-to-text conversion?**

- A) Azure Translator
- B) Azure Cognitive Services – Speech
- C) Azure Machine Learning
- D) Azure Bot Services
- **Answer**: B

26. **Which of the following would be a good use case for Azure Form Recognizer?**

- A) Classifying images based on pre-trained models
- B) Extracting structured data from forms and documents
- C) Building predictive models for customer churn
- D) Converting speech to text
- **Answer**: B

27. **What is the function of Azure's Custom Vision service?**

- A) It automatically recognizes objects and faces in images.
- B) It allows users to train custom image classification models.
- C) It provides translations for images.
- D) It performs speech-to-text conversion on images.

- **Answer**: B

28. **What is Azure Databricks primarily used for?**

- A) To deploy AI models at scale
- B) To store large datasets for AI models
- C) To collaborate on data science and machine learning projects
- D) To process real-time data streams
- **Answer**: C

29. **Which Azure service allows the creation of custom, low-code chatbots that can be integrated with messaging platforms like Microsoft Teams?**

- A) Azure Cognitive Services – Speech API
- B) Azure Bot Services
- C) Azure Translator
- D) Azure Machine Learning
- **Answer**: B

30. **What is the primary benefit of using Azure Cognitive Services' Speech SDK?**

- A) To transcribe and analyze audio files
- B) To convert audio to text and vice versa, in real time
- C) To store speech data securely
- D) To manage speech data workflows
- **Answer**: B

31. **Which Azure service would you use to recognize handwriting in an image?**

- A) Azure Cognitive Services – Computer Vision
- B) Azure Bot Services
- C) Azure Translator

- D) Azure Speech Services
- **Answer**: A

32. **In Azure, which of the following is used for real-time language translation in multiple languages?**

- A) Azure Translator
- B) Azure Language Understanding (LUIS)
- C) Azure Cognitive Search
- D) Azure Form Recognizer
- **Answer**: A

33. **What is the function of Azure's Language Understanding (LUIS)?**

- A) Speech recognition
- B) Text analysis and sentiment detection
- C) Understanding the intent behind user queries in natural language
- D) Translating languages
- **Answer**: C

34. **Which Azure service helps you automate and scale machine learning models using containers?**

- A) Azure Kubernetes Service (AKS)
- B) Azure Cognitive Services
- C) Azure Bot Services
- D) Azure Machine Learning
- **Answer**: A

35. **What is a key feature of Azure Cognitive Services' Face API?**

- A) Detecting emotions from text

- B) Recognizing and analyzing faces in images
- C) Generating captions for videos
- D) Translating text into different languages
- **Answer**: B

36. **Which of the following Azure services can be used to analyze sentiment in text?**

- A) Azure Text Analytics API
- B) Azure Speech Services
- C) Azure Custom Vision
- D) Azure Bot Services
- **Answer**: A

37. **In Azure Machine Learning, what is the primary function of a Jupyter notebook?**

- A) To store large datasets for analysis
- B) To manage the deployment of machine learning models
- C) To write and execute code for data analysis and machine learning
- D) To visualize machine learning model performance
- **Answer**: C

38. **What does the Azure AI service Personalizer help you achieve?**

- A) Providing personalized experiences for users based on their preferences
- B) Translating multiple languages in real-time
- C) Performing sentiment analysis on customer feedback
- D) Detecting objects in images
- **Answer**: A

39. **Which of the following services helps build custom image classification models in Azure?**

- A) Azure Custom Vision
- B) Azure Bot Services
- C) Azure Cognitive Search
- D) Azure Machine Learning
- **Answer**: A

40. **What is the role of Azure Key Vault in AI solutions?**

- A) It stores large datasets for machine learning.
- B) It manages and protects sensitive information like API keys and credentials.
- C) It helps in model training.
- D) It provides a graphical interface for machine learning applications.
- **Answer**: B

41. **Which of the following can Azure Cognitive Services' Text Analytics API NOT do?**

- A) Perform sentiment analysis
- B) Extract key phrases from text
- C) Recognize faces in images
- D) Detect language from text
- **Answer**: C

42. **Which Azure service would you use to detect anomalies in a set of time-series data?**

- A) Azure Anomaly Detector
- B) Azure Machine Learning
- C) Azure Cognitive Search

- D) Azure Speech Services
- **Answer**: A

43. **Which of the following AI technologies in Azure is used for creating intelligent conversational agents?**

- A) Azure Bot Services
- B) Azure Cognitive Services – Face API
- C) Azure Machine Learning
- D) Azure Personalizer
- **Answer**: A

44. **Which of the following services is used to identify topics from a given set of documents?**

- A) Azure Text Analytics API
- B) Azure Language Understanding (LUIS)
- C) Azure Cognitive Search
- D) Azure Personalizer
- **Answer**: C

45. **What is the key benefit of integrating Azure Machine Learning with Azure Kubernetes Service (AKS)?**

- A) It reduces the cost of model deployment.
- B) It enables scaling of machine learning models to handle large datasets.
- C) It allows automatic translation of models to multiple languages.
- D) It simplifies the process of training models with complex data.
- **Answer**: B

46. **Which Azure service provides capabilities for text translation and transliteration?**

- A) Azure Translator

- B) Azure Text Analytics

- C) Azure Speech Services

- D) Azure Custom Vision

- **Answer**: A

47. **Which of the following is a feature of Azure Cognitive Services' Speech API?**

- A) Translating speech into multiple languages

- B) Recognizing images in videos

- C) Converting spoken words into text in real-time

- D) Extracting sentiment from text

- **Answer**: C

48. **What is Azure Machine Learning used for?**

- A) Building and deploying custom AI models

- B) Providing pre-built machine learning models

- C) Automating tasks using pre-built workflows

- D) Performing sentiment analysis on text data

- **Answer**: A

49. **Which of the following services would you use to perform handwriting recognition on a document?**

- A) Azure Cognitive Services – Computer Vision

- B) Azure Translator

- C) Azure Bot Services

- D) Azure Language Understanding (LUIS)

- **Answer**: A

50. **Which Azure service would you use to manage and orchestrate multiple AI models in a scalable way?**

- A) Azure Kubernetes Service (AKS)
- B) Azure Cognitive Services
- C) Azure Machine Learning
- D) Azure Databricks
- **Answer:** A

51. **Which of the following services would be best suited for creating a recommendation system for a retail website?**

- A) Azure Machine Learning
- B) Azure Cognitive Services – Text Analytics
- C) Azure Personalizer
- D) Azure Bot Services
- **Answer:** C

52. **Which of the following is NOT a feature of the Azure Cognitive Services Face API?**

- A) Detecting human faces in images
- B) Identifying the age and gender of people in images
- C) Recognizing emotions in faces
- D) Generating captions for images
- **Answer:** D

53. **What does Azure Cognitive Services' Translator API provide?**

- A) Sentiment analysis of text in multiple languages
- B) Speech recognition in multiple languages
- C) Text translation between supported languages

- D) Image captioning
- **Answer**: C

54. **Which Azure service would you use to detect and analyze emotions in text data?**

- A) Azure Text Analytics
- B) Azure Cognitive Search
- C) Azure Language Understanding (LUIS)
- D) Azure Cognitive Services – Face API
- **Answer**: A

55. **Which of the following services is best suited for managing large, unstructured datasets for machine learning applications?**

- A) Azure Cognitive Services – Computer Vision
- B) Azure Blob Storage
- C) Azure Databricks
- D) Azure Synapse Analytics
- **Answer**: B

56. **Which Azure service would you use for scaling AI model deployments in a containerized environment?**

- A) Azure Machine Learning
- B) Azure Kubernetes Service (AKS)
- C) Azure Cognitive Services
- D) Azure Databricks
- **Answer**: B

57. **Which of the following is an example of a cognitive service available in Azure?**

- A) Azure Blob Storage
- B) Azure Databricks
- C) Azure Cognitive Services – Speech
- D) Azure Synapse Analytics
- **Answer**: C

58. **Which of the following is NOT a use case for Azure Cognitive Services' Speech API?**

- A) Speech-to-text conversion
- B) Text-to-speech conversion
- C) Recognizing entities in text
- D) Real-time translation of speech
- **Answer**: C

59. **Which Azure service would you use to extract structured information, like names and dates, from a document?**

- A) Azure Text Analytics
- B) Azure Form Recognizer
- C) Azure Cognitive Search
- D) Azure Personalizer
- **Answer**: B

60. **What is the role of Azure's Custom Vision service in AI model development?**

- A) It helps in training custom image classification models.
- B) It provides automatic translation for images.
- C) It recognizes faces and objects in images.
- D) It analyzes the sentiment of text data.
- **Answer**: A

61. **In Azure, which of the following services would you use to train and deploy deep learning models?**

- A) Azure Cognitive Services
- B) Azure Machine Learning
- C) Azure Personalizer
- D) Azure Bot Services
- **Answer**: B

62. **Which of the following Azure services is best suited for analyzing large amounts of unstructured text data?**

- A) Azure Cognitive Services – Text Analytics
- B) Azure Cognitive Services – Computer Vision
- C) Azure Machine Learning
- D) Azure Databricks
- **Answer**: A

63. **Which of the following would be most appropriate for building a conversational agent that understands user intents and entities?**

- A) Azure Machine Learning
- B) Azure Bot Services and Language Understanding (LUIS)
- C) Azure Personalizer
- D) Azure Translator
- **Answer**: B

64. **What does Azure's Language Understanding (LUIS) primarily focus on?**

- A) Image recognition
- B) Translating text into multiple languages
- C) Understanding natural language and user intent

- D) Sentiment analysis
- **Answer**: C

65. **What is the main feature of Azure's Form Recognizer?**

- A) To analyze sentiment in text data
- B) To extract structured data from forms and documents
- C) To recognize objects and faces in images
- D) To translate text into different languages
- **Answer**: B

66. **Which Azure service would you use for detecting anomalies in time-series data?**

- A) Azure Anomaly Detector
- B) Azure Cognitive Services – Face API
- C) Azure Databricks
- D) Azure Cognitive Search
- **Answer**: A

67. **Which Azure service allows you to build, train, and deploy models for natural language processing (NLP)?**

- A) Azure Cognitive Services – Text Analytics
- B) Azure Machine Learning
- C) Azure Bot Services
- D) Azure Translator
- **Answer**: B

68. **What is the primary use of Azure Kubernetes Service (AKS) in AI?**

- A) To build and train machine learning models

- B) To scale the deployment of machine learning models
- C) To translate text in real-time
- D) To analyze large datasets
- **Answer**: B

69. **What is the purpose of Azure Cognitive Services' Speech SDK?**

- A) To build custom NLP models
- B) To convert speech into text and vice versa
- C) To manage and scale machine learning models
- D) To store sensitive speech data securely
- **Answer**: B

70. **Which of the following services would you use to create multilingual chatbots?**

- A) Azure Cognitive Services – Text Analytics
- B) Azure Bot Services with Language Understanding (LUIS)
- C) Azure Translator
- D) Azure Personalizer
- **Answer**: B

71. **Which service would you use to build and deploy custom machine learning models on Azure?**

- A) Azure Cognitive Services
- B) Azure Machine Learning
- C) Azure Bot Services
- D) Azure Databricks
- **Answer**: B

72. **What is the primary function of Azure Cognitive Services' Language API?**

- A) Text translation
- B) Sentiment analysis and key phrase extraction
- C) Object detection in images
- D) Speech-to-text conversion
- **Answer**: B

73. **Which of the following services would be most useful for analyzing the sentiment of customer reviews in text?**

- A) Azure Text Analytics
- B) Azure Cognitive Services – Face API
- C) Azure Databricks
- D) Azure Personalizer
- **Answer**: A

74. **What does Azure Cognitive Services' Computer Vision API allow you to do?**

- A) Perform speech-to-text conversion
- B) Recognize and analyze visual content in images
- C) Extract key phrases from text
- D) Build predictive models
- **Answer**: B

75. **Which of the following tools is best suited for analyzing large datasets using machine learning algorithms?**

- A) Azure Databricks
- B) Azure Cognitive Services
- C) Azure Bot Services
- D) Azure Synapse Analytics
- **Answer**: A

76. **What does the Azure Bot Framework enable developers to do?**

- A) Build conversational agents that can be integrated with messaging platforms
- B) Analyze the sentiment of conversations
- C) Convert text into speech
- D) Detect entities in text
- **Answer**: A

77. **What does Azure's Custom Vision service allow developers to do?**

- A) Perform object detection and classification in images
- B) Create conversational AI bots
- C) Translate text into different languages
- D) Generate insights from large datasets
- **Answer**: A

78. **Which Azure service can be used to deploy an AI model as an API for easy integration with other services?**

- A) Azure Cognitive Services
- B) Azure Kubernetes Service (AKS)
- C) Azure Machine Learning
- D) Azure Cognitive Search
- **Answer**: C

79. **What is the purpose of Azure Cognitive Services' Language API for named entity recognition (NER)?**

- A) To detect and categorize entities such as people, organizations, and locations in text
- B) To perform sentiment analysis on text

- C) To recognize objects in images
- D) To convert speech to text
- **Answer**: A

80. **Which of the following is the best way to scale AI model deployment using Azure?**

- A) Using Azure Kubernetes Service (AKS) for containerized deployment
- B) Using Azure Bot Services for conversational bots
- C) Using Azure Cognitive Services for real-time analysis
- D) Using Azure Machine Learning for training models
- **Answer**: A

81. **Which of the following services allows you to build predictive models by using Azure Machine Learning Studio?**

- A) Azure Cognitive Services
- B) Azure Databricks
- C) Azure Machine Learning Designer
- D) Azure Bot Services
- **Answer**: C

82. **Which Azure service is best suited for analyzing time-series data for anomaly detection?**

- A) Azure Anomaly Detector
- B) Azure Synapse Analytics
- C) Azure Cognitive Search
- D) Azure Machine Learning
- **Answer**: A

83. In Azure, what is the best tool to manage machine learning lifecycle, including training, testing, and deploying models?

- A) Azure Machine Learning Studio
- B) Azure Cognitive Services
- C) Azure Databricks
- D) Azure Synapse Analytics
- **Answer**: A

84. Which of the following Azure services can be used to store sensitive speech data securely?

- A) Azure Key Vault
- B) Azure Blob Storage
- C) Azure Cognitive Services
- D) Azure Storage Accounts
- **Answer**: A

85. Which of the following is used for content moderation in videos and images through Azure Cognitive Services?

- A) Azure Text Analytics
- B) Azure Content Moderator
- C) Azure Personalizer
- D) Azure Machine Learning
- **Answer**: B

86. What feature does Azure's Face API provide for facial recognition?

- A) Emotion detection
- B) Text recognition in images
- C) Object detection

- D) Speech recognition
- **Answer**: A

87. Which of the following is an example of using Azure Cognitive Services to automate customer service interactions?

- A) Using the Face API to verify user identity
- B) Using Text Analytics for sentiment analysis in customer feedback
- C) Using Azure Translator to translate website content
- D) Using Azure Bot Services to deploy a chatbot
- **Answer**: D

88. How can you extend Azure Bot Services for voice interaction?

- A) Use Azure Machine Learning to generate text-based models
- B) Integrate with Azure Cognitive Services' Speech API for voice recognition
- C) Use Azure Databricks for real-time voice interaction analysis
- D) Integrate with Azure Cognitive Services' Text Analytics API
- **Answer**: B

89. What is a benefit of using Azure Kubernetes Service (AKS) for AI model deployment?

- A) Automatically scales and manages the AI model containers
- B) Prepares data for analysis using Azure Synapse Analytics
- C) Provides real-time text translation
- D) Deploys models for predictive analytics
- **Answer**: A

90. Which Azure service should you use to manage API keys securely when building AI-powered applications?

- A) Azure Active Directory
- B) Azure Key Vault
- C) Azure Cognitive Services
- D) Azure Blob Storage
- **Answer**: B

91. Which service would be most appropriate for conducting speech-to-text conversion in real time?

- A) Azure Cognitive Services – Speech
- B) Azure Language Understanding (LUIS)
- C) Azure Databricks
- D) Azure Cognitive Search
- **Answer**: A

92. Which of the following is an example of a task that can be performed using Azure Cognitive Services' Text Analytics API?

- A) Object detection
- B) Sentiment analysis
- C) Speech-to-text conversion
- D) Image classification
- **Answer**: B

93. What Azure service can be used to deploy machine learning models at scale with automatic scaling of workloads?

- A) Azure Cognitive Services
- B) Azure Machine Learning
- C) Azure Kubernetes Service (AKS)
- D) Azure Databricks
- **Answer**: C

94. What is the function of Azure's Personalizer service?

- A) Provide real-time translation services
- B) Personalize recommendations based on user behavior
- C) Enable voice recognition in conversational bots
- D) Detect and classify objects in images
- **Answer**: B

95. Which of the following services can be used to classify and extract data from scanned documents?

- A) Azure Form Recognizer
- B) Azure Cognitive Services – Face API
- C) Azure Personalizer
- D) Azure Translator
- **Answer**: A

96. Which of the following is a responsibility of the Azure Security Center when securing AI solutions?

- A) Ensuring compliance with data privacy regulations
- B) Encrypting sensitive data in Azure Blob Storage
- C) Automating the deployment of machine learning models
- D) Monitoring and identifying security vulnerabilities across resources
- **Answer**: D

97. Which service would you use to analyze customer feedback for sentiment analysis and identify key topics?

- A) Azure Cognitive Services – Text Analytics
- B) Azure Machine Learning
- C) Azure Databricks

- D) Azure Cognitive Services – Speech API
- **Answer**: A

98. How would you integrate custom NLP models into your Azure solution?

- A) By using Azure Cognitive Services – Text Analytics
- B) By using Azure Machine Learning and deploying as APIs
- C) By using Azure Databricks for real-time analysis
- D) By using Azure Logic Apps for workflow automation
- **Answer**: B

99. Which of the following Azure services would you use for real-time conversational AI solutions?

- A) Azure Cognitive Services – Text Analytics
- B) Azure Machine Learning
- C) Azure Bot Services
- D) Azure Databricks
- **Answer**: C

100. Which feature in Azure Cognitive Services would you use to translate text into multiple languages?

- A) Azure Translator
- B) Azure Personalizer
- C) Azure Cognitive Search
- D) Azure Language Understanding (LUIS)
- **Answer**: A

101. Which service would you use to create conversational AI applications that can understand and process natural language commands?

- A) Azure Bot Services
- B) Azure Machine Learning
- C) Azure Cognitive Services – Text Analytics
- D) Azure Language Understanding (LUIS)
- **Answer**: D

102. Which of the following is an important consideration when designing a chatbot solution using Azure Bot Services?

- A) Implementing a highly scalable database
- B) Managing role-based access control (RBAC)
- C) Integrating with multiple communication channels
- D) Using Azure Functions for long-running tasks
- **Answer**: C

103. What is the primary purpose of the Azure Cognitive Services – Computer Vision API?

- A) To convert text to speech
- B) To identify objects, text, and landmarks in images
- C) To analyze and process video data
- D) To provide sentiment analysis of text
- **Answer**: B

104. Which of the following Azure services would you use for secure API management?

- A) Azure Cognitive Services
- B) Azure API Management
- C) Azure Functions
- D) Azure Databricks
- **Answer**: B

105. How can Azure Machine Learning service assist with deploying models for inference at scale?

- A) By using the Azure Cognitive Services API to handle predictions
- B) By leveraging Azure Kubernetes Service (AKS) for scalable deployment
- C) By processing data using Azure Synapse Analytics
- D) By managing bot dialogues and user intents in Azure Bot Services
- **Answer**: B

106. Which Azure tool would you use to preprocess data and train machine learning models using a graphical user interface (GUI)?

- A) Azure Machine Learning Designer
- B) Azure Cognitive Services
- C) Azure Databricks
- D) Azure Bot Services
- **Answer**: A

107. Which service would you use to extract information from structured documents such as invoices, receipts, and forms?

- A) Azure Form Recognizer
- B) Azure Cognitive Services – Speech
- C) Azure Text Analytics
- D) Azure Bot Services
- **Answer**: A

108. What type of AI model is most appropriate for a recommendation engine in Azure?

- A) Object detection models
- B) Time-series forecasting models

- C) Collaborative filtering models
- D) Image classification models
- **Answer:** C

109. Which Azure service would you use to manage security, compliance, and data privacy in AI solutions?

- A) Azure Key Vault
- B) Azure Security Center
- C) Azure Machine Learning
- D) Azure Cognitive Services – Text Analytics
- **Answer:** B

110. Which Azure service should you use to handle multiple languages in a speech-to-text solution?

- A) Azure Cognitive Services – Translator
- B) Azure Cognitive Services – Speech to Text
- C) Azure Cognitive Services – Language Understanding (LUIS)
- D) Azure Databricks
- **Answer:** B

111. When scaling an AI model in Azure, which of the following is a critical factor for ensuring performance at scale?

- A) Minimize the number of cloud resources
- B) Optimize models for latency and throughput
- C) Use only pre-trained models for scalability
- D) Restrict access to APIs and models to a single user
- **Answer:** B

112. What Azure feature can help you manage and protect sensitive data when implementing AI solutions?

- A) Azure Security Center
- B) Azure Key Vault
- C) Azure Cognitive Services
- D) Azure Resource Manager
- **Answer**: B

113. Which Azure service would you use to deploy custom machine learning models built in Python or R?

- A) Azure Machine Learning
- B) Azure Bot Services
- C) Azure Databricks
- D) Azure Functions
- **Answer**: A

114. Which of the following is a common use case for Azure's Speech Services?

- A) Real-time speech-to-text transcription
- B) Image classification in photos
- C) Text summarization from documents
- D) Object detection in video streams
- **Answer**: A

115. Which tool in Azure would you use to orchestrate AI workflows involving multiple services?

- A) Azure Logic Apps
- B) Azure Databricks
- C) Azure Bot Services

- D) Azure Functions
- **Answer**: A

116. What should you do to ensure that AI solutions comply with regulations such as GDPR?

- A) Implement a secure authentication mechanism in Azure AD
- B) Use Azure Synapse Analytics for compliance monitoring
- C) Use Microsoft's Responsible AI Framework for compliance and transparency
- D) Encrypt data with Azure Storage Encryption
- **Answer**: C

117. Which Azure Cognitive Services API should you use to analyze and extract insights from customer feedback in the form of text?

- A) Azure Language Understanding (LUIS)
- B) Azure Text Analytics
- C) Azure Cognitive Search
- D) Azure Computer Vision
- **Answer**: B

118. Which Azure service can help improve the accuracy of your natural language processing models by providing large-scale labeled datasets for training?

- A) Azure Cognitive Services – Text Analytics
- B) Azure Machine Learning
- C) Azure Bot Services
- D) Azure Databricks
- **Answer**: B

119. What feature does Azure Cognitive Services offer to identify and classify emotions in faces in images?

- A) Face API
- B) Custom Vision API
- C) Text Analytics API
- D) Personalizer API
- **Answer**: A

120. Which Azure service can help you manage and monitor the performance of deployed machine learning models in production?

- A) Azure Machine Learning
- B) Azure Synapse Analytics
- C) Azure Cognitive Services – Face API
- D) Azure Monitor
- **Answer**: A

121. Which of the following is true about using Azure's Custom Vision API?

- A) It can automatically train models for image classification
- B) It requires users to manually label the data for training
- C) It supports text classification tasks only
- D) It is only available in the premium tier of Azure Cognitive Services
- **Answer**: A

122. Which of the following is the primary benefit of using Azure Databricks for AI model development?

- A) It simplifies API management
- B) It provides an environment for large-scale data processing and collaboration

- C) It helps with speech-to-text applications
- D) It directly integrates with Azure Key Vault for data encryption
- **Answer**: B

123. Which of the following is a primary use of Azure's Text Analytics API?

- A) Recognizing objects in images
- B) Translating text between languages
- C) Analyzing sentiment and extracting key phrases from text
- D) Speech-to-text conversion
- **Answer**: C

124. Which Azure service can you use to securely share machine learning models with external partners or teams?

- A) Azure Key Vault
- B) Azure Blob Storage
- C) Azure Machine Learning
- D) Azure Active Directory
- **Answer**: C

125. In a conversational AI system, which of the following is responsible for maintaining the state of the conversation between the bot and the user?

- A) Dialog Management
- B) Cognitive Services
- C) Azure Active Directory
- D) Language Understanding (LUIS)
- **Answer**: A

126. Which of the following is a key feature of Azure Cognitive Services - Custom Vision API?

- A) It supports only text-based tasks.
- B) It allows you to train custom models for image classification.
- C) It automatically generates scripts for deployment.
- D) It can generate real-time transcription of speech.
- **Answer**: B

127. When you deploy a machine learning model using Azure Machine Learning, what is the default environment for running inference tasks?

- A) Virtual Machines
- B) Kubernetes Cluster
- C) Azure App Services
- D) Azure Container Instances
- **Answer**: D

128. Which Azure service would you use to handle multiple speech-to-text requests at a global scale?

- A) Azure Kubernetes Service (AKS)
- B) Azure Cognitive Services – Speech
- C) Azure Active Directory
- D) Azure Synapse Analytics
- **Answer**: B

129. Which of the following tools does Azure provide for developing custom AI models?

- A) Azure Cognitive Services - Text Analytics
- B) Azure Machine Learning Studio
- C) Azure Logic Apps
- D) Azure Monitor
- **Answer**: B

130. Which of the following is true about Azure Speech Services?

- A) It supports only speech-to-text conversion.
- B) It provides a suite of speech-related APIs, including text-to-speech, speech-to-text, and speech translation.
- C) It requires users to manually define voice models.
- D) It is intended solely for video analytics.
- **Answer**: B

131. In Azure Bot Services, which tool can you use to analyze and improve a bot's performance using real-world interactions?

- A) Azure Synapse Analytics
- B) Azure Machine Learning Studio
- C) Bot Analytics in Azure Bot Services
- D) Azure Monitor
- **Answer**: C

132. How can you improve the performance of your machine learning models in Azure Machine Learning?

- A) By manually writing training scripts
- B) By using Azure AI accelerated hardware like GPUs and FPGAs
- C) By scaling to a higher-tier subscription
- D) By using only pre-trained models from Azure
- **Answer**: B

133. What is the primary use of Azure Text Analytics API?

- A) Analyzing customer feedback
- B) Identifying and extracting objects from images
- C) Managing API keys and secrets

- D) Converting speech into text
- **Answer**: A

134. What is a key consideration when deploying AI models in production environments at scale in Azure?

- A) Restricting the use of third-party libraries
- B) Ensuring that the models can scale automatically based on demand
- C) Implementing a manual deployment process
- D) Using only CPU-based hardware for cost efficiency
- **Answer**: B

135. Which Azure feature allows you to optimize and test different versions of your machine learning model to identify the most effective one?

- A) Azure Kubernetes Service (AKS)
- B) Azure Machine Learning Designer
- C) Azure Machine Learning – Model Registry
- D) Azure Cognitive Search
- **Answer**: C

136. What is the purpose of the Azure Cognitive Services Personalizer API?

- A) It allows you to train custom models for object detection.
- B) It enables personalized content delivery based on user interactions.
- C) It analyzes text for sentiment and key phrases.
- D) It enables natural language understanding for bots.
- **Answer**: B

137. Which service allows for automatic scaling of deployed machine learning models to accommodate varying traffic levels?

- A) Azure Cognitive Services
- B) Azure Databricks
- C) Azure Machine Learning
- D) Azure Bot Services
- **Answer**: C

138. Which service in Azure is best suited for automating workflows that involve AI-driven processes?

- A) Azure Functions
- B) Azure Logic Apps
- C) Azure Kubernetes Service (AKS)
- D) Azure Cognitive Services
- **Answer**: B

139. Which of the following can help you manage sensitive information such as API keys and passwords in Azure?

- A) Azure Key Vault
- B) Azure Functions
- C) Azure Monitor
- D) Azure Active Directory
- **Answer**: A

140. What does Azure Cognitive Services – Computer Vision API do?

- A) It helps with extracting text from scanned images and PDF documents.
- B) It analyzes sentiment in images and videos.
- C) It detects objects, text, and facial emotions in images.
- D) It manages the security of AI models.
- **Answer**: C

141. Which tool allows you to test and debug your conversational AI models built in Azure Bot Services?

- A) Bot Framework Emulator
- B) Azure Functions
- C) Azure Machine Learning Studio
- D) Azure DevOps
- **Answer**: A

142. In Azure, which service would you use to implement real-time translation of speech in multiple languages?

- A) Azure Translator
- B) Azure Cognitive Services – Text Analytics
- C) Azure Cognitive Services – Speech Translation
- D) Azure Synapse Analytics
- **Answer**: C

143. Which of the following can help ensure AI models in Azure comply with regulatory requirements such as GDPR and HIPAA?

- A) Azure Security Center
- B) Microsoft's Responsible AI Framework
- C) Azure Kubernetes Service (AKS)
- D) Azure Logic Apps
- **Answer**: B

144. When implementing speech recognition in a multi-channel application, which Azure service would you use to handle the translation of voice commands in real-time?

- A) Azure Cognitive Services – Speech API

- B) Azure Bot Services
- C) Azure Active Directory
- D) Azure Synapse Analytics
- **Answer**: A

145. Which Azure service would be most useful for an organization looking to create a customized AI model for classifying and tagging medical images?

- A) Azure Machine Learning
- B) Azure Cognitive Services – Custom Vision
- C) Azure Databricks
- D) Azure Key Vault
- **Answer**: B

146. What is a key feature of Azure Cognitive Services – Translator?

- A) It provides real-time speech-to-speech translation.
- B) It automatically generates machine learning models.
- C) It translates written text into multiple languages.
- D) It provides natural language understanding.
- **Answer**: C

147. What role does Azure Kubernetes Service (AKS) play in deploying AI solutions?

- A) It enables the creation of custom bots for applications.
- B) It manages API keys and credentials for secure AI applications.
- C) It facilitates the deployment and management of containerized AI applications at scale.
- D) It offers a pre-built solution for predictive analytics.
- **Answer**: C

148. Which of the following services would you use to train and deploy machine learning models in a scalable and efficient manner in Azure?

- A) Azure Databricks
- B) Azure Cognitive Services – Computer Vision
- C) Azure Machine Learning
- D) Azure Functions
- **Answer**: C

149. Which tool would you use to automate the deployment of AI models into Azure environments?

- A) Azure Logic Apps
- B) Azure DevOps
- C) Azure Active Directory
- D) Azure Cognitive Services – Language Understanding
- **Answer**: B

150. Which Azure service allows you to monitor and analyze the behavior of deployed AI models in real time?

- A) Azure Monitor
- B) Azure Cognitive Services – Text Analytics
- C) Azure Databricks
- D) Azure Bot Services
- **Answer**: A

151. Which of the following tools in Azure helps monitor and maintain AI models deployed for inference?

- A) Azure Monitor
- B) Azure Kubernetes Service (AKS)

- C) Azure Functions
- D) Azure Cognitive Search
- **Answer**: A

152. What Azure service is used to develop, train, and deploy machine learning models with a focus on scalability and performance?

- A) Azure Machine Learning
- B) Azure Databricks
- C) Azure DevOps
- D) Azure Synapse Analytics
- **Answer**: A

153. Which service in Azure can be used for real-time sentiment analysis of customer feedback?

- A) Azure Cognitive Services – Text Analytics
- B) Azure Bot Services
- C) Azure Cognitive Services – Computer Vision
- D) Azure Machine Learning
- **Answer**: A

154. Which of the following is the primary benefit of using Azure Cognitive Services for AI applications?

- A) It requires no machine learning expertise.
- B) It provides pre-built AI models that can be customized for specific use cases.
- C) It only works for text-based AI tasks.
- D) It enables on-premises AI model training.
- **Answer**: B

155. Which of the following Azure services is specifically designed for analyzing and processing video and image content?

- A) Azure Cognitive Services – Computer Vision
- B) Azure Machine Learning
- C) Azure Bot Services
- D) Azure Key Vault
- **Answer**: A

156. Which feature of Azure Cognitive Services – Custom Vision allows the classification of images based on custom labels?

- A) Image Tagging
- B) Object Detection
- C) Custom Training
- D) Optical Character Recognition (OCR)
- **Answer**: C

157. In Azure Cognitive Services, which service would be best for translating user input from one language to another in a chatbot application?

- A) Azure Translator
- B) Azure Cognitive Services – Speech API
- C) Azure Language Understanding (LUIS)
- D) Azure Cognitive Services – Text Analytics
- **Answer**: A

158. What is the role of Azure Kubernetes Service (AKS) in AI model deployment?

- A) It provides the infrastructure for training AI models.
- B) It enables auto-scaling and container orchestration for AI model deployment.

- C) It is used for training natural language models.
- D) It hosts AI model databases and reports.
- **Answer**: B

159. What type of AI model is primarily used for understanding and generating human language in Azure AI solutions?

- A) Recurrent Neural Networks (RNNs)
- B) Generative Adversarial Networks (GANs)
- C) Natural Language Processing (NLP) models
- D) Decision Trees
- **Answer**: C

160. Which Azure service enables the development of custom machine learning models for computer vision tasks such as object detection and image classification?

- A) Azure Cognitive Services – Custom Vision
- B) Azure Machine Learning
- C) Azure Databricks
- D) Azure Logic Apps
- **Answer**: A

161. Which Azure service is useful for automating machine learning model training and testing pipelines?

- A) Azure DevOps
- B) Azure Machine Learning
- C) Azure Logic Apps
- D) Azure Databricks
- **Answer**: B

162. Which of the following is NOT a common use case for Azure Cognitive Services – Text Analytics?

- A) Sentiment analysis of customer reviews
- B) Translation of text to different languages
- C) Key phrase extraction from documents
- D) Identification of entities in unstructured text
- **Answer**: B

163. Which of the following Azure services enables building AI-powered chatbots that can handle real-time conversations?

- A) Azure Cognitive Services – Text Analytics
- B) Azure Bot Services
- C) Azure Speech Services
- D) Azure Machine Learning
- **Answer**: B

164. Which Azure service is specifically designed to enable the development of end-to-end AI workflows with minimal coding?

- A) Azure Logic Apps
- B) Azure Cognitive Services
- C) Azure Databricks
- D) Azure Synapse Analytics
- **Answer**: A

165. Which Azure service would you use to monitor the performance and health of your deployed AI models?

- A) Azure Monitor
- B) Azure Synapse Analytics

- C) Azure Cognitive Services – Computer Vision
- D) Azure Bot Services
- **Answer**: A

166. Which of the following services would you use to securely manage keys, secrets, and certificates needed for AI applications?

- A) Azure Key Vault
- B) Azure Active Directory
- C) Azure Cognitive Services – Language Understanding (LUIS)
- D) Azure Cognitive Services – Translator
- **Answer**: A

167. Which of the following services is used to automate the deployment of AI models and workflows in Azure?

- A) Azure DevOps
- B) Azure Logic Apps
- C) Azure Machine Learning
- D) Azure Functions
- **Answer**: A

168. What does Azure Cognitive Services – Language Understanding (LUIS) enable?

- A) It processes text and converts it to speech.
- B) It enables natural language understanding for building conversational AI applications.
- C) It translates text from one language to another.
- D) It performs image recognition tasks.
- **Answer**: B

169. In Azure Cognitive Services, which service is used for speech-to-text conversion?

- A) Azure Cognitive Services – Text Analytics
- B) Azure Cognitive Services – Speech API
- C) Azure Cognitive Services – Language Understanding (LUIS)
- D) Azure Cognitive Services – Translator
- **Answer**: B

170. What role does Azure Synapse Analytics play in AI-driven workflows?

- A) It manages API keys for AI models.
- B) It processes and analyzes large datasets, which can be used for training AI models.
- C) It automatically deploys machine learning models.
- D) It monitors AI model performance.
- **Answer**: B

171. In which Azure service can you define and manage a set of AI-based workflows for automating business tasks?

- A) Azure Logic Apps
- B) Azure Machine Learning
- C) Azure Cognitive Services – Speech
- D) Azure Databricks
- **Answer**: A

172. Which Azure service allows for efficient real-time text translation across multiple languages in a chatbot?

- A) Azure Translator
- B) Azure Cognitive Services – Computer Vision

- C) Azure Language Understanding (LUIS)
- D) Azure Speech Services
- **Answer**: A

173. What Azure service would you use for training and managing machine learning models with automated ML capabilities?

- A) Azure Machine Learning
- B) Azure Cognitive Services
- C) Azure Bot Services
- D) Azure Databricks
- **Answer**: A

174. Which of the following services helps you integrate machine learning models into an enterprise solution using APIs?

- A) Azure Machine Learning
- B) Azure Functions
- C) Azure Logic Apps
- D) Azure API Management
- **Answer**: D

175. Which service in Azure provides pre-built models for recognizing entities, such as people, places, or products, in text?

- A) Azure Cognitive Services – Text Analytics
- B) Azure Machine Learning
- C) Azure Cognitive Services – Language Understanding (LUIS)
- D) Azure Cognitive Services – Computer Vision
- **Answer**: A

176. What tool can be used to deploy machine learning models as web services in Azure?

- A) Azure Cognitive Services
- B) Azure Machine Learning
- C) Azure Functions
- D) Azure Synapse Analytics
- **Answer**: B

177. What type of machine learning model would you likely use for a sentiment analysis task?

- A) Regression model
- B) Classification model
- C) Clustering model
- D) Generative model
- **Answer**: B

178. Which of the following Azure services would you use to perform optical character recognition (OCR) on scanned documents?

- A) Azure Cognitive Services – Computer Vision
- B) Azure Cognitive Services – Text Analytics
- C) Azure Machine Learning
- D) Azure Bot Services
- **Answer**: A

179. What is a primary benefit of using Azure Databricks for AI development?

- A) It provides an easy-to-use interface for building and deploying AI models.
- B) It integrates seamlessly with Azure Machine Learning and facilitates big data processing.

- C) It automates the training of machine learning models.
- D) It offers pre-trained models for image analysis.
- **Answer**: B

180. Which service allows you to train and deploy speech recognition models in Azure?

- A) Azure Cognitive Services – Speech API
- B) Azure Cognitive Services – Text Analytics
- C) Azure Synapse Analytics
- D) Azure Bot Services
- **Answer**: A

181. Which of the following is a core benefit of using Azure Cognitive Services for AI tasks?

- A) It requires high-level machine learning expertise.
- B) It allows you to use pre-trained models to solve common AI tasks without writing custom code.
- C) It only supports AI tasks related to text processing.
- D) It enables running AI models on on-premises environments.
- **Answer**: B

182. Which Azure service provides a pre-built framework for building conversational AI applications?

- A) Azure Bot Services
- B) Azure Cognitive Services – Language Understanding (LUIS)
- C) Azure Cognitive Services – Speech API
- D) Azure Machine Learning
- **Answer**: A

183. Which Azure service provides the capability to recognize and categorize objects in images?

- A) Azure Cognitive Services – Computer Vision
- B) Azure Cognitive Services – Text Analytics
- C) Azure Cognitive Services – Language Understanding (LUIS)
- D) Azure Synapse Analytics
- **Answer**: A

184. Which Azure service is used for the training, management, and deployment of custom machine learning models?

- A) Azure Machine Learning
- B) Azure Databricks
- C) Azure Cognitive Services – Computer Vision
- D) Azure Logic Apps
- **Answer**: A

185. What is the main purpose of Azure Cognitive Services – Text Analytics?

- A) To analyze images and recognize objects
- B) To extract sentiment, key phrases, and named entities from text
- C) To translate text between languages
- D) To identify speech and convert it to text
- **Answer**: B

186. Which of the following is a key consideration when using Azure Cognitive Services for real-time speech recognition in an application?

- A) Ensuring that the system has a high-level understanding of the context of the speech
- B) Real-time translation from one language to another

- C) Securing the speech data using Azure Active Directory
- D) Providing the ability to recognize multiple speakers simultaneously
- **Answer**: A

187. Which service in Azure would be most appropriate for building a recommendation system for a retail website?

- A) Azure Machine Learning
- B) Azure Cognitive Services – Text Analytics
- C) Azure Cognitive Services – Computer Vision
- D) Azure Synapse Analytics
- **Answer**: A

188. Which of the following tools can be used to monitor and analyze the performance of deployed machine learning models in Azure?

- A) Azure Monitor
- B) Azure Cognitive Services – Language Understanding (LUIS)
- C) Azure Databricks
- D) Azure Logic Apps
- **Answer**: A

189. In Azure Cognitive Services, which feature allows you to analyze written text to extract key phrases and named entities?

- A) Text Analytics API
- B) Translator API
- C) Speech API
- D) Language Understanding (LUIS)
- **Answer**: A

190. Which Azure service would you use to detect and interpret faces in images?

- A) Azure Cognitive Services – Computer Vision
- B) Azure Cognitive Services – Face API
- C) Azure Cognitive Services – Text Analytics
- D) Azure Bot Services
- **Answer**: B

191. Which Azure service enables you to integrate AI-powered capabilities, such as text analysis and machine learning, directly into your application workflows?

- A) Azure Logic Apps
- B) Azure Synapse Analytics
- C) Azure Cognitive Services
- D) Azure DevOps
- **Answer**: A

192. Which Azure service is most commonly used to recognize and categorize objects in video content?

- A) Azure Cognitive Services – Computer Vision
- B) Azure Cognitive Services – Face API
- C) Azure Cognitive Services – Video Indexer
- D) Azure Machine Learning
- **Answer**: C

193. Which Azure service provides the ability to extract and understand context from unstructured text, including customer queries?

- A) Azure Cognitive Services – Language Understanding (LUIS)
- B) Azure Machine Learning
- C) Azure Cognitive Services – Speech API
- D) Azure Cognitive Services – Translator
- **Answer**: A

194. What is the primary purpose of Azure Machine Learning Designer?

- A) To enable AI and machine learning workflows with minimal coding
- B) To create and train deep learning models for computer vision tasks
- C) To manage cloud infrastructure for machine learning workloads
- D) To monitor deployed machine learning models
- **Answer**: A

195. Which Azure service can be used to deploy and manage AI models as REST APIs for integration with applications?

- A) Azure Machine Learning
- B) Azure Databricks
- C) Azure Bot Services
- D) Azure Cognitive Services
- **Answer**: A

196. Which of the following services allows you to process large datasets, like log files and social media data, for sentiment analysis?

- A) Azure Cognitive Services – Text Analytics
- B) Azure Machine Learning
- C) Azure Synapse Analytics
- D) Azure Logic Apps
- **Answer**: C

197. What feature of Azure Machine Learning allows for version control of machine learning models?

- A) Azure DevOps Integration
- B) Model Registry
- C) Azure Cognitive Services Integration

- D) Azure Active Directory
- **Answer**: B

198. Which of the following is NOT a benefit of using Azure Cognitive Services for AI solutions?

- A) Simplified integration with existing applications
- B) Access to pre-trained models for common AI tasks
- C) Requires building custom models for every use case
- D) Scalable API usage for production applications
- **Answer**: C

199. Which service is designed to support and build large-scale AI and machine learning models for big data workloads in Azure?

- A) Azure Databricks
- B) Azure Cognitive Services
- C) Azure Logic Apps
- D) Azure Synapse Analytics
- **Answer**: A

200. Which service would you use to build and deploy scalable conversational AI solutions that can understand and process customer inquiries?

- A) Azure Bot Services
- B) Azure Cognitive Services – Speech API
- C) Azure Language Understanding (LUIS)
- D) Azure Cognitive Services – Text Analytics
- **Answer**: A

201. Which of the following is the main focus of Azure Cognitive Services – Face API?

- A) Detecting and recognizing faces in images
- B) Translating speech into text
- C) Performing sentiment analysis on text
- D) Generating text responses in conversations
- **Answer**: A

202. What is the role of Azure Cognitive Services – Translator API in a multilingual application?

- A) It transcribes audio into multiple languages.
- B) It translates text from one language to another.
- C) It provides text-to-speech conversion.
- D) It analyzes the sentiment of multilingual text.
- **Answer**: B

203. Which Azure service helps you create and manage machine learning pipelines for automating model deployment and monitoring?

- A) Azure DevOps
- B) Azure Machine Learning
- C) Azure Databricks
- D) Azure Synapse Analytics
- **Answer**: B

204. Which service allows you to train custom machine learning models without writing code?

- A) Azure Machine Learning Designer
- B) Azure Cognitive Services – Custom Vision
- C) Azure Logic Apps
- D) Azure Synapse Analytics
- **Answer**: A

205. In Azure, which of the following would be best for implementing secure and scalable deployment of AI models?

- A) Azure Kubernetes Service (AKS)
- B) Azure Functions
- C) Azure Logic Apps
- D) Azure Synapse Analytics
- **Answer**: A

206. Which service in Azure is primarily used for speech synthesis and speech recognition?

- A) Azure Cognitive Services – Speech API
- B) Azure Cognitive Services – Text Analytics
- C) Azure Cognitive Services – Translator
- D) Azure Bot Services
- **Answer**: A

207. Which of the following is a feature of Azure Cognitive Services – Custom Vision?

- A) It allows users to analyze speech patterns.
- B) It helps users create custom image classification models.
- C) It provides pre-trained models for natural language understanding.
- D) It provides real-time video processing capabilities.
- **Answer**: B

208. Which Azure service is most suitable for automating workflows involving AI tasks like data extraction and document processing?

- A) Azure Logic Apps
- B) Azure Cognitive Services – Text Analytics

- C) Azure Cognitive Services – Computer Vision
- D) Azure Machine Learning
- **Answer**: A

209. Which Azure service helps users manage the security of sensitive data, such as AI model secrets and training data?

- A) Azure Key Vault
- B) Azure Active Directory
- C) Azure DevOps
- D) Azure Logic Apps
- **Answer**: A

210. Which Azure tool is used for creating scalable, cloud-based machine learning models and big data solutions?

- A) Azure Databricks
- B) Azure Cognitive Services
- C) Azure Synapse Analytics
- D) Azure Logic Apps
- **Answer**: A

211. Which of the following is a core benefit of using Azure Cognitive Services for text-to-speech functionality?

- A) It allows for real-time translation between languages.
- B) It provides speech recognition for multiple languages.
- C) It converts text into speech in a natural-sounding voice.
- D) It transcribes speech into text.
- **Answer**: C

212. Which Azure service is most appropriate for developing a highly customized image recognition system for a unique set of images?

- A) Azure Cognitive Services – Custom Vision
- B) Azure Cognitive Services – Computer Vision
- C) Azure Machine Learning
- D) Azure Bot Services
- **Answer**: A

213. Which Azure service can help you detect anomalies in time-series data, such as sensor readings or transaction data?

- A) Azure Machine Learning
- B) Azure Anomaly Detector
- C) Azure Cognitive Services – Text Analytics
- D) Azure Logic Apps
- **Answer**: B

214. Which of the following services allows you to build, train, and deploy conversational agents or bots?

- A) Azure Cognitive Services – Speech API
- B) Azure Machine Learning
- C) Azure Bot Services
- D) Azure Cognitive Services – Text Analytics
- **Answer**: C

215. What does Azure Cognitive Services – Translator API primarily focus on?

- A) Converting speech into text
- B) Converting text into speech
- C) Translating text between different languages

- D) Identifying key phrases in text
- **Answer**: C

216. Which of the following Azure services allows you to customize and extend the functionality of bots by adding custom code and skills?

- A) Azure Bot Services
- B) Azure Cognitive Services – Language Understanding (LUIS)
- C) Azure Cognitive Services – Speech API
- D) Azure Machine Learning
- **Answer**: A

217. Which feature of Azure Machine Learning provides version control for datasets used in training machine learning models?

- A) Data Drift
- B) Dataset Registry
- C) Model Registry
- D) Pipeline Versioning
- **Answer**: B

218. Which of the following is true regarding the use of Azure Cognitive Services – Language Understanding (LUIS)?

- A) It allows you to build conversational agents capable of understanding natural language input.
- B) It requires a significant amount of custom code to integrate into applications.
- C) It only works with pre-trained models for basic tasks.
- D) It is used exclusively for analyzing text sentiment.
- **Answer**: A

219. Which of the following is a primary feature of Azure Cognitive Services – Face API?

- A) Detecting faces in images and recognizing emotions
- B) Converting speech into text
- C) Translating text between multiple languages
- D) Analyzing time-series data for anomalies
- **Answer**: A

220. Which Azure service is best suited for building AI-driven applications that analyze and process unstructured data from documents?

- A) Azure Cognitive Services – Form Recognizer
- B) Azure Cognitive Services – Text Analytics
- C) Azure Machine Learning
- D) Azure Logic Apps
- **Answer**: A

221. Which service would you use to deploy an AI model as a REST API in Azure for integration with client applications?

- A) Azure Machine Learning
- B) Azure Cognitive Services – Computer Vision
- C) Azure Databricks
- D) Azure Synapse Analytics
- **Answer**: A

222. What is the purpose of Azure Cognitive Services – Custom Vision?

- A) To analyze video content for object detection
- B) To create custom image classification models tailored to a specific business need

- C) To analyze speech data for sentiment
- D) To translate text between languages
- **Answer**: B

223. Which service allows you to process large volumes of speech data and convert it to text in real-time?

- A) Azure Cognitive Services – Speech-to-Text
- B) Azure Cognitive Services – Text Analytics
- C) Azure Cognitive Services – Translator
- D) Azure Cognitive Services – Speech API
- **Answer**: A

224. Which of the following Azure services is most appropriate for integrating machine learning models into business workflows?

- A) Azure Logic Apps
- B) Azure Databricks
- C) Azure Synapse Analytics
- D) Azure Machine Learning
- **Answer**: A

225. What is the primary benefit of using Azure Cognitive Services for AI tasks?

- A) Requires no cloud integration
- B) Provides pre-trained models for common AI tasks, reducing the need for custom model training
- C) Only works with specific types of AI applications like robotics
- D) Requires complex coding skills for integration
- **Answer**: B

226. Which Azure service allows you to deploy machine learning models to the cloud and monitor their performance?

- A) Azure Machine Learning
- B) Azure Bot Services
- C) Azure Synapse Analytics
- D) Azure Cognitive Services
- **Answer**: A

227. Which of the following services provides pre-built models for processing and understanding human speech?

- A) Azure Cognitive Services – Speech API
- B) Azure Cognitive Services – Text Analytics
- C) Azure Cognitive Services – Language Understanding (LUIS)
- D) Azure Cognitive Services – Translator
- **Answer**: A

228. Which Azure service is used to analyze and understand video content by extracting insights such as facial recognition and scene classification?

- A) Azure Cognitive Services – Video Indexer
- B) Azure Cognitive Services – Computer Vision
- C) Azure Cognitive Services – Face API
- D) Azure Machine Learning
- **Answer**: A

229. Which service should be used to manage the lifecycle of machine learning models, including version control and deployment?

- A) Azure Machine Learning
- B) Azure Synapse Analytics

- C) Azure DevOps
- D) Azure Cognitive Services – Computer Vision
- **Answer**: A

230. What is the key feature of Azure Cognitive Services – Speech-to-Text API?

- A) It converts text into speech in real time.
- B) It transcribes spoken language into written text.
- C) It analyzes emotions in speech data.
- D) It translates speech between languages.
- **Answer**: B

231. Which Azure service is used for extracting structured data from forms, such as invoices or receipts?

- A) Azure Cognitive Services – Form Recognizer
- B) Azure Cognitive Services – Computer Vision
- C) Azure Cognitive Services – Text Analytics
- D) Azure Cognitive Services – Speech API
- **Answer**: A

232. What Azure service allows you to create automated workflows for AI-related tasks like document processing or customer data analysis?

- A) Azure Logic Apps
- B) Azure Databricks
- C) Azure Machine Learning
- D) Azure Cognitive Services – Speech API
- **Answer**: A

233. Which of the following is a primary function of Azure Cognitive Services – Language Understanding (LUIS)?

- A) Translating text into other languages

- B) Analyzing the sentiment of text

- C) Extracting key phrases from text

- D) Enabling a chatbot to understand and process user queries

- **Answer**: D

234. Which service can be used to monitor the performance of AI models deployed on Azure?

- A) Azure Monitor

- B) Azure Synapse Analytics

- C) Azure Cognitive Services – Text Analytics

- D) Azure Logic Apps

- **Answer**: A

235. Which of the following is a primary use case for Azure Cognitive Services – Computer Vision?

- A) Translating spoken language to text

- B) Analyzing and extracting text from images

- C) Converting text into speech

- D) Understanding and categorizing customer queries

- **Answer**: B

236. Which Azure service would you use to build a recommendation system for a media streaming application?

- A) Azure Machine Learning

- B) Azure Cognitive Services – Text Analytics

- C) Azure Cognitive Services – Computer Vision

- D) Azure Synapse Analytics

- **Answer**: A

237. Which Azure service allows you to build custom AI models for image recognition based on your own dataset?

- A) Azure Cognitive Services – Custom Vision
- B) Azure Cognitive Services – Face API
- C) Azure Cognitive Services – Text Analytics
- D) Azure Cognitive Services – Speech API
- **Answer**: A

238. Which Azure service allows you to securely store and manage sensitive data such as API keys and connection strings used in AI solutions?

- A) Azure Key Vault
- B) Azure Active Directory
- C) Azure Machine Learning
- D) Azure Logic Apps
- **Answer**: A

239. Which of the following is NOT a benefit of using Azure Cognitive Services?

- A) Pre-trained models for various AI tasks
- B) Ease of integration into applications with REST APIs
- C) Ability to write custom machine learning algorithms
- D) Simplified authentication and security management
- **Answer**: C

240. Which Azure service can be used to deploy scalable AI models and services in a Kubernetes-based environment?

- A) Azure Kubernetes Service (AKS)
- B) Azure DevOps
- C) Azure Synapse Analytics

- D) Azure Logic Apps
- **Answer**: A

241. What is the primary purpose of Azure Cognitive Services – Speech API?

- A) To enable real-time speech-to-text transcription
- B) To translate speech from one language to another
- C) To analyze sentiment in audio files
- D) To recognize and categorize images in videos
- **Answer**: A

242. Which of the following is a use case for Azure Cognitive Services – Text Analytics?

- A) Object recognition in images
- B) Translating text to speech
- C) Analyzing sentiment and extracting key phrases from text
- D) Managing speech data for transcription
- **Answer**: C

243. Which Azure service would you use for real-time translation of speech data into text?

- A) Azure Cognitive Services – Speech-to-Text
- B) Azure Cognitive Services – Translator
- C) Azure Cognitive Services – Speech API
- D) Azure Bot Services
- **Answer**: A

244. Which service allows you to use pre-trained AI models for detecting faces, identifying emotions, and analyzing facial features in images?

- A) Azure Cognitive Services – Face API
- B) Azure Cognitive Services – Computer Vision
- C) Azure Cognitive Services – Custom Vision
- D) Azure Cognitive Services – Text Analytics
- **Answer**: A

245. Which of the following Azure services would you use to process and analyze video data for insights?

- A) Azure Cognitive Services – Video Indexer
- B) Azure Cognitive Services – Speech API
- C) Azure Cognitive Services – Text Analytics
- D) Azure Cognitive Services – Computer Vision
- **Answer**: A

246. Which of the following is a primary use case for Azure Cognitive Services – Language Understanding (LUIS)?

- A) Speech-to-text transcription
- B) Text translation
- C) Intent recognition and entity extraction from natural language input
- D) Object detection in images
- **Answer**: C

247. Which Azure service allows you to build and deploy machine learning models with minimal code and no infrastructure management?

- A) Azure Machine Learning Studio
- B) Azure Cognitive Services – Text Analytics
- C) Azure Synapse Analytics
- D) Azure DevOps
- **Answer**: A

248. Which Azure service provides pre-trained models for text translation in multiple languages?

- A) Azure Cognitive Services – Translator
- B) Azure Cognitive Services – Language Understanding (LUIS)
- C) Azure Cognitive Services – Text Analytics
- D) Azure Cognitive Services – Computer Vision
- **Answer**: A

249. Which service would you use to monitor and track the performance of AI models and algorithms deployed on Azure?

- A) Azure Monitor
- B) Azure Logic Apps
- C) Azure Synapse Analytics
- D) Azure Machine Learning
- **Answer**: A

250. Which of the following Azure services can be used for the creation of custom machine learning models that involve large-scale image data processing?

- A) Azure Cognitive Services – Custom Vision
- B) Azure Machine Learning
- C) Azure Cognitive Services – Computer Vision
- D) Azure Databricks
- **Answer**: B